USEFUL PHRASES IN THE SHANGHAI DIALECT

This edition published by Lector House in 2024

ISBN: 978-93-5800-826-5

Lector House LLP
Registered Office: H. No. 96, Block C, Tomar Colony,
Burari, Delhi – 110084, India
info@lectorhouse.com
www.lectorhouse.com

USEFUL PHRASES IN THE SHANGHAI DIALECT

GILBERT MCINTOSH

2024

LECTOR HOUSE LLP

USEFUL PHRASES IN THE SHANGHAI DIALECT

WITH INDEX-VOCABULARY AND OTHER HELPS

COMPILED BY

GILBERT MCINTOSH

SECOND EDITION

Contents

Introduction

THE compilation of these phrases was suggested by the frequent requests on the part of busy residents or transient visitors for a handbook containing easily-learned every-day words and phrases. The compiler is well aware that there is no royal road or short cut to learning, and would recommend to those who have the time for the more thorough study of the colloquial a careful study of Dr. Hawks Pott's "Lessons in the Shanghai Dialect" (or Dr. Yates' First Lessons in Chinese), and a constant use of the Shanghai Vocabulary, as well as the excellent Chinese-English Dictionary prepared by Messrs. Silsby and Davis.

We trust that these phrases will not only be of immediate use to the busy housewife and merchant, or inquiring tourist, but will be of effective assistance to the student in the acquisition of a knowledge of the idiom. The Chinese mode of thought and method of speech differs so largely from our own that the acquirement of a fluent and familiar use of colloquial Chinese seems only possible by committing to memory, or carefully studying, such sentences as are collected in the following pages. A useful practice would be to rewrite the English word by word, according to the order in the vernacular, so as to perceive the construction of sentences and the peculiar use of verbs, adverbs, prepositions, connective and terminal particles, etc. To aid in the recognition of the English equivalents of the Chinese character or romanised we have added an index and vocabulary of the words used in this book. This will require to be used cautiously, as the meanings given in many cases are not the primary ones, but rather those used in certain phrases. It ought also to be mentioned that the grammatical and topical groups at the end of the book are not complete, but are added for convenience of reference and in the hope that they will tempt to a fuller study through the medium of the more elaborate works.

The description of the romanised system used is reproduced, by kind permission, from the material supplied by Rev. J. A. Silsby to accompany the romanised translation of the Police Regulations published by the Shanghai Municipal Council. This system of romanisation was adopted by the Shanghai Vernacular Society in 1899, and has many merits, not the least being the absence of diacritical marks.

Grateful thanks are accorded to friends who have helped with advice, particularly to Rev. G. F. Fitch, D.D., Rev. J. A. Silsby, and Mr. Kau Voong-dz (高鳳池). Such help was very necessary from the manner in which various native teachers differed as to pronunciation and idiom.

In spite of all the pains taken in the preparation of these sentences and in the revision for this second edition it is possible that errors still remain; the compiler, therefore, will be grateful for corrections, which will be duly noted in prospect of a possible future edition.

G. M.

Shanghai, 23rd March, 1908.

Description of the Shanghai Romanised System.

Nearly all the syllables are represented by the combination of an initial and a final, a system which has been found to be well adapted to the Chinese language.

Initials.

The UPPER SERIES are—*p*, *'m*, *'v*, *t*, *ts*, *s*, *'l*, *'ny*, *'ng*, *k*, *ky*, *kw*, *i* and *'w*. These initials are pronounced in most cases much the same as in English, but without aspiration, higher in pitch and with very little vibration of the larynx. The apostrophe before a letter indicates that the letter belongs to the "higher series." Pure vowel initials also belong to this series.

'ny has a sound similar to that of *ni* in spa*ni*el.

ky = *ch* in *ch*uk with all aspiration eliminated.

i as an initial has the sound of *i* in dahlia.

The ASPIRATES are—*ph*, *f*, *th*, *tsh*, *kh*, *ch*, *khw*, *h*, *hy*, and *hw* (*th* as in *Th*omson—not as in *th*ing).

ch = *ch* in *ch*urch.

hy is nearly like *ti* in Por*ti*a.

The other aspirates are like the corresponding initials of the higher series with the addition of a strong aspiration (indicated by *h*).

The LOWER SERIES are—*b*, *m*, *v*, *d*, *dz*, *z*, *l*, *n*, *ny*, *ng*, *g*, *j*, *gw*, *y*, and *w*. Their pronunciation is much the same as in English. They are lower in pitch than corresponding initials of the "higher series," and have more "voice," being pronounced with more decided vibration of the larynx. The lower vowel initials, indicated by an inverted comma (‘) and attended with a slight aspiration, belong to this series.

Finals.

1. The Vowel Endings are—*a*, *e*, *i*, *au*, *o*, *oo*, *oe*, *eu*, *u*, *ui*, *ia*, *iau*, *ieu*, and *ie*.

2. The Nasal Endings are—(*a*) *an*, *en*, *ien* and *oen*, in which the *n* is not sounded, but lengthens out and imparts a nasal quality to the preceding vowel; (*b*) *ang*, *aung*, *oong*, (or *ong*), *ung* and *iang*, in which *ng* has the value of *ng* in so*ng*, but is often nearer the French *n* in *bon*; (*c*) *uin*, in which *n* is sonant and has a value varying between *n* and *ng*.

3. The Abrupt Vowel Endings are—*ak*, *ah*, *eh*, *ih*, *auh*, *ok*, *oeh*, *uh*, and *iak*, in which *h* and *k* are the signs of the *zeh-sung* (入聲), and the vowel is pronounced in a short, abrupt manner.

The sounds of the vowels are—

a as in f*a*r, except when followed by *n* or *h*, when it has the sound of *a* in m*a*n or m*a*t.

e as in pr*e*y; before *h* it has the sound of *e* as in m*e*t.

i as in capr*i*ce; before *h* or *ng* it is shortened to *i* as in m*i*t or s*i*ng.

au as in *Au*gust.

o or *oo* as *ou* in th*ou*gh or in thr*ou*gh. It is really a combination of these two sounds, and is modified by its environment.

oe as in G*oe*the (German ö).

eu as in French Monsi*eu*r.

u as in oo in f*oo*t (always preceded by an *s* sound).

ui as in in fr*ui*t (or rather French ü).

In *ia*, *iau*, *ieu* and *ie*, we have short *i* followed closely by *a*, *au*, *eu*, and *e*, as described above.

Of course it is understood that the Chinese sounds in a majority of cases vary somewhat from the English sounds which are given as the nearest equivalent.

The Dok-yoong Z-moo— "Init ial s *used alone*" i.e., without vowels, are—*ts*, *tsh*, *dz*, *s*, *z*, *an*, *ng*, and *r*. The first five are followed by the vowel sound in the second syllable of *able*—prolonged. Mateer and Bailer use ï for this sound and the new Mandarin Romanized uses ï̤. It is not written, but understood in the Shanghai system. *m* has the sound of *m* in chas*m* and *ng* the sound of *ng* in ha*ng*er; *r* is a sound between final *r* and *l*.

Tone Marks.—As in Ningpo and other Woo dialects, tone marks are unnecessary in ordinary letter-press, and are omitted in this book.

Salutations.

Good morning.

早呀 *Tsau-'a,* 儂早 *Noong tsau.*

How are you? (are you well?)

好拉否 *Hau la va?*

Sir, may I ask your name? [to a gentleman, equal, or superior].

貴姓 or 尊姓 *Kwe-sing?* (or) *Tsung-sing?*

What is your name? (surname) [to workmen, coolies, etc.]

儂姓啥 *Noong sing sa?*

My humble name [polite form] is Gold.

敝姓金 *Bi sing Kyung.*

My name is Gold, [ordinary].

我姓金 *Ngoo sing Kyung.*

What is your "given" name? [polite form].

大號是啥 *Da-'au z sa?*

What is your "given" name? [ordinary].

儂个名頭叫啥

Noong-kuh ming-deu kyau sa?

My "given" name is John [polite form].

賤號約翰 *Dzien 'au Iak-'oen.*

My "given" name is John. [ordinary].

我个名頭呌約翰

Ngoo-kuh ming-deu kyau Iak-'oen.

Sir, may I ask your age? [polite].

先生貴庚 *Sien-sang kwe-kang?*

How old are you? [ordinary].

儂幾歲 *Noong kyi soe?*

I am thirty years old [polite form].

虛度三十歲 *Hyui doo san-seh soe.*

I am thirty years old. [ordinary].

我三十歲 *Ngoo san-seh soe.*

To-day is cold.

今朝是冷 *Kyung-tsau z lang.*

To-day is very warm.

今朝蠻暖熱 *Kyung-tsau 'man noen-nyih.*

To-day is hot.

今朝頂熱 *Kyung-tsau ting nyih.*

There is much wind to-day.

今朝風大 *Kyung-tsau foong doo.*

It is raining to-day.

今朝落雨 *Kyung-tsau lauh-yui.*

It is beautiful weather to-day.

今朝天氣蠻好

Kyung-tsau thien-chi 'man-hau.

Recently we have had too much rain.

近來雨水忒多

Jung-le yui-s thuh-too.

It has been too dry.

近來天氣忒旱

Jung-le thien-chi thuh 'oen.

What have you come for?

儂來啥尊幹 (or) 儂來啥事體

Noong le sa tsung-koen, (or) *noong le sa z-thi.*

Come again in two days.

等兩日再來 *Tung liang nyih tse-le.*

Take a cup of tea.

請用一杯茶 *Tshing yoong ih-pe dzo.*

Thank you.

謝謝 *Zia-zia.*

Do you smoke?

濃吃烟否 *Noong chuh-ien va?*

No, thank you, I do not smoke.

謝謝，我勿吃 *Zia-zia, ngoo 'veh chuh.*

Is business good?

儂个生意好否 *Noong-kuh sang-i hau va?*

It is bad.

勿好 *'Veh hau.*

It is fairly good.

還好 *Wan hau.*

It is very good.

蠻好 *'Man-hau.*

Is your friend well?

儂个朋友好拉否

Noong-kuh bang-yeu hau la va?

He is sick.

伊垃拉生病 *Yi leh-la sang-bing.*

Good-bye (said by person leaving).

少陪儂 *Sau be noong.*

Good-bye (said to person leaving).

慢去 *Man chi* or *man man chi* (lit., go slowly).

Good-bye (expecting to meet later on).

晏歇會 *An hyih we.*

Good-bye (we meet to-morrow).

明朝會 *Ming-tsau we.*

Good-bye (we meet again).

再會 *Tse we.*

Good-bye (we meet after some days).

間 (or 隔) 日會 *Kan* (or *kak*) *nyih we.*

The following anticipate ordinary queries from a Chinese visitor:—

What is your honorable country?

貴國是那裡一國

Kwe kok z 'a-li ih kok?

My humble country is England.

敝國是英國 *Bi kok z Iung-kok.*

The following are more colloquial in style:—

I am an Englishman.

我是英國人

Ngoo z Iung-kok nyung.

I am an American.

我是美國人 (or 花旗人)

Ngoo z 'Me-kok nyung (or *Hwo-ji nyung*).

I am a German.

我是德國人 *Ngoo z Tuh-kok nyung.*

I am a Frenchman.

我是法國人 *Ngoo z Fah-kok nyung.*

When did you come to China?

幾時到中國个

Kyi-z tau Tsoong-kok kuh?

I came fifteen years ago.

我 (已經) 來之十五年哉

Ngoo (i-kyung) le-ts so-ng nyien tse.

Upon what business did you come to China?

儂到中國來做啥

Noong tau Tsoong-kok le tsoo sa?

I am a merchant.

我是生意人

Ngoo z sang-i-nyung.

I am a doctor.

我是醫生

Ngoo z i-sang.

I am a missionary.

我是傳道个

Ngoo z dzen-dau kuh.

I am merely visiting.

我來是遊歷个

Ngoo le z yeu-lih kuh.

I am a commercial traveller.

我來是兜生意个

Ngoo le z teu sang-i kuh.

I am a ship's officer.

我拉輪船上辦事个

Ngoo la lung-zen laung ban z kuh.

Have you a wife?

儂已經成親否 (or) 儂有娘子否

Noong i-kyung dzung-tshing va? (or) *noong yeu nyang-ts va?*

Yes, she is in England.

我有个,伊現在拉英國

Ngoo yeu kuh; yi yien-dze la Iung-kok.

Yes, she is coming soon.
伊就要來快哉
Yi zieu iau le khwa tse.

Have you any children?
儂有啥小囝否
Noong yeu sa siau noen va?

Three sons and two daughters.
我有三个兒子咾兩个囝
Ngoo yeu san-kuh nyi-ts lau liang-kuh noen.

What age are they?
伊拉幾歲哉
Yi-la kyi soe tse?

The oldest is 20 years old.
頂大个是念歲
Ting doo kuh z nyan soe.

The youngest is 12 years old.
頂小个是十二歲
Ting-siau-kuh z zeh-nyi soe.

Give my greetings to your family,
望望儂个一家門
Maung-maung noong-kuh ih ka-mung.

On the Street.

Ricksha, come!

東洋車 (or) 東洋車來

Toong-yang-tsho (or) *toong-yang-tsho le!*

Go ahead.

朝前 (or) 走上去

Dzau-zien (or) *tseu-zaung chi.*

Go to the right.

到右邊去 *Tau yeu-pien chi.*

Go to the left.

到左邊去 *Tau tsi-pien chi.*

Go back.

回轉去 *We-tsen chi.*

Wait here.

等拉 (or) 等拉第頭

Tung la (or) *tung la di-deu.*

I want to go to the Hongkong and Shanghai Bank.

我要到滙豐銀行去

Ngoo iau tau We-foong nyung-'aung chi.

I want to go to the German Bank.

我要到德華銀行去

Ngoo iau tau Tuh-wo nyung-'aung chi.

I want to go to the Imperial Customs.

我要到新關去

Ngoo iau tau Sing-kwan chi.

I want to go to the Astor House.

我要到禮查去

Ngoo iau tau Li-dzo chi.

I want to go to the Club.

我要到總會去

Ngoo iau tau Tsoong-we chi.

I want to go to the Railway Station.

我要到火車站去

Ngoo iau tau hoo-tsho dzan chi.

I want to go to the Steamer Jetty.

我要到輪船碼頭去

Ngoo iau tau lung-zen mo-deu chi.

I do not know the way; take me to the Police Office.

我勿認得路;儂車我到巡捕房去

Ngoo 'veh nyung-tuh loo; noong tsho ngoo tau Dzing-boo-vaung chi.

[I have paid] enough.

有哉 (or) 彀哉 *Yeu-tse* (or) *Keu-tse.*

[What I have paid you is] not too little.

勿少拉哉 *'Veh sau la tse.*

I have already paid you according to custom.

我已經照規矩付儂

Ngoo i-kyung tsau kwe-kyui foo noong.

Go quicker.

跑來快點 . *Bau-le khwa-tien.*

Go slower.

跑來慢點 *Bau-le man-tien.*

Stop.

停 (or) 停下來 *Ding* (or) *Ding-'au-le.*

Stop for a little while.

停一停 *Ding-ih-ding.*

[Because of rain] put up the hood.

[爲之落雨]篷布撑起來

[*We-ts lauh-yui*] *boong-poo tshang-chi-le.*

Put the hood back.

蓬布放下去 *Boong-poo faung-'au-chi.*

Have you a waterproof apron?

油布有否 *Yeu-poo yeu va?*

Please tell me where the bank is?

請告訴我銀行拉那裡

Tshing kau-soo ngoo nyung-'aung la 'a-li?

Please tell me where Chinese books can be bought.

請告訴我那裡可以買中國書

Tshing kau-soo ngoo 'a-li khau-i ma Tsoong-kok su.

Please tell me where Foreign books can be bought.

請告訴我外國書那裡好買

Tshing kau-soo ngoo nga-kok su 'a-li hau ma?

Please tell me where foreign clothes can be bought.

請告訴我外國衣裳那裡好買

Tshing kau-soo ngoo nga-kok i-zaung ‘a-li hau ma?

Please tell me where there is an eating house or (hotel).

請告訴我那裡有外國飯店 (or 客寓)

Tshing kau-soo ngoo ‘a-li yeu nga-kok van-tien (or *khak-nyui*).

Take me to the British Consulate.

車我到大英公館去

Tsho ngoo tau Da-Iung koong-kwen chi.

Take me to the American Consulate.

車我到花旗公館去

Tsho ngoo tau Hwo-ji koong-kwen chi.

Take me to the Cathedral.

車我到紅禮拜堂去

Tsho ngoo tau ‘Oong-li-pa-daung chi.

Take me to Union Church.

車我到蘇州河禮拜堂去

Tsho ngoo tau Soo-tseu-‘oo li-pa-daung chi.

Still another (ricksha) is wanted.

還要一部

wan iau ih boo.

Can this parcel go into the ricksha?

第个包子車子上擺得落否

Di-kuh pau-ts tsho-ts laung pa-tuh-lauh va?

For other useful directions see section on “Direction.”

The Merchant.

Have you any business to-day?

今朝儂有啥事體否

Kyung-tsau noong yeu sa z-thi va?

Do you wish to order anything to-day?

今朝儂要定啥貨色否

Kyung-tsau noong iau ding[1] *sa hoo-suh va?*

Yes, I want to order.[2]

我要定个

Ngoo iau ding kuh.

I do not want to order.

我勿要定啥貨

Ngoo 'veh iau ding sa hoo.

I want to purchase.

我要買 *Ngoo iau ma.*

---

[1] *Ding* (定) and *Ta* (帶) are commonly used in Shanghai as equivalents for "order." *Ding* actually contains the idea of contract and money paid; *Ta* actually contains the idea of bringing the goods with you; but they each have a wider significance.

[2] *Ding* (定) and *Ta* (帶) are commonly used in Shanghai as equivalents for "order." *Ding* actually contains the idea of contract and money paid; *Ta* actually contains the idea of bringing the goods with you; but they each have a wider significance.

I want to sell.

我要賣脫 *Ngoo iau ma-theh.*

It cannot be bought (i.e., Can not sell at that price).

買勿動 *Ma 'veh doong.*

It can be bought (i.e., Can sell at that price).

買得動 (or 可以買)

Ma tuh-doong (or *Khau-i ma*).

What do you want to buy?

儂要買啥物事

Noong iau ma sa meh-z?

Will you sell?

儂要賣脫否 *Noong iau ma-theh va?*

What is the price of this?

第个啥價錢 *Di-kuh sa ka-dien?*

[This] price is too dear.

價錢忒貴 *Ka-dien thuh kyui.*

When will the goods come?

貨色幾時到 *Hoo-suh kyi-z tau?*

If too late I cannot use them.

若是忒慢我用勿著

Zak-z thuh man, ngoo yoong-'veh-dzak.

These goods are worse than last time.

第回个貨色比上次㑚 (or 退班)

Di-we kuh hoo-suh pi zaung ths cheu (or the-pan).

To-day I have goods to be imported.

今朝我有貨色進口

Kyung-tsau ngoo yeu hoo-suh tsing-kheu.

To-day I have goods to export.

今朝我有貨色出口

Kyung-tsau ngoo yeu hoo-suh tsheh-kheu.

To-day I have goods to tranship.

今朝我有貨色過船

Kyung-tsau ngoo yeu hoo-suh koo-zen.

To-day I have goods to re-export.

今朝我有貨色轉口

Kyung-tsau ngoo yeu hoo-suh tsen-kheu.

How much duty on these goods?

第个貨色要完幾化稅

Di-kuh hoo-suh iau wen kyi-hau soe?

Has the Duty Memo come?

稅單有來否 *Soe-tan yeu le va?*

Have you received the Duty Memo?

稅單儂收着末 *Soe-tan noong seu-dzak meh?*

[Duty Memo] has not come yet.

[稅單]還勿曾到 *Wan 'veh-zung tau.*

Duty has been paid.

稅已經完拉哉 *Soe i-kyung wen la tse.*

Duty has not been paid.

稅勿曾完過 *Soe 'veh-zung wen-koo.*

Please pay your duty.

請完儂个稅 *Tshing wen noong-kuh soe.*

Make out the Import application.

要預備進口單 *Iau yui-be tsing-kheu-tan.*

Make out the Export application.

要預備出口單 *Iau yui-be tsheh-kheu-tan.*

Take delivery of the goods at once.

貨色就要提轉來

Hoo-suh zieu iau di-tsen-le.

Put these goods in the godown.

貨色可以寄拉棧房裡

Hoo-suh khau-i kyi la dzan-vaung-li.

When one's own godown is meant, 上 *zaung* is used in place of 寄 *kyi.*

Is there any storage?

要啥棧租否

Iau sa dzan-tsoo va?

How much storage is there?

要幾化棧租 *Iau kyi-hau dzan-tsoo?*

Among them, four bales are damaged by water; I cannot receive them.

內中四件有水濕个,我勿能收

Ne-tsong-s-jien yeu s sah-kuh; ngoo 'veh-nung seu.

You brought the delivery order too late, therefore I cannot pay storage.

儂提單送來忒晏,所以我勿能付棧租

Noong di-tan soong le thuh-an, soo-i ngoo 'veh-nung foo dzan-tsoo.

The goods are now at Pootung.

貨色現在拉浦東

Hoo-suh yien-dze la Phoo-toong.

Do you want a Customs Pass?

儂要派司否 *Noong iau pha-s va?*

Yes, I want one.

要个 *Iau-kuh.*

No, I do not want any.

勿要 *'Veh iau.*

How many passes do you want?

儂要幾張派司 *Noong iau kyi tsang pha-s?*

I want one pass.

我要一張派司 *Ngoo iau ih-tsang pha-s.*

I want two passes.

我要兩張派司 *Ngoo iau liang-tsang pha-s.*

Please put my goods through the Customs quickly.

我个貨色請儂快點報關

Ngoo-kuh hoo-suh tshing noong khwa-tien pau kwan.

Has the steamer arrived?

輪船到未 *Lung-zen tau meh?*

When will the steamer arrive?

輪船幾時到 *Lung-zen kyi-z tau?*

What is the name of the steamer?

輪船个名頭叫啥

Lung-zen-kuh ming-deu kyau sa?

To what Company does the steamer belong?

啥人家行裡个輪船

Sa-nyung-ka 'aung-li-kuh lung-zen?

At what wharf is she discharging?

拉那裏一个碼頭卸貨

La 'a-li ih-kuh mo-deu sia-hoo?

At Hongkew (Jardine's) Wharf.

拉虹口怡和碼頭

La 'Oong-kheu Yi-woo Mo-deu.

At Pootung Wharf.
拉浦東碼頭 *La Phoo-toong Mo-deu.*

At China Merchants' Lower Wharf.
拉招商局北棧碼頭
La Tsau-saung jok Pok-dzan Mo-deu.

At Yangtze Wharf.
拉揚子碼頭 *La Yang-ts Mo-deu.*

At Old Ningpo Wharf.
拉老甯波碼頭 *La Lau Nyung-poo Mo-deu.*

What are your shipping marks?
倗个記號 [or 墨頭] 是啥
Na-kuh kyi-'au [or *muh-deu*] *z sa?*

To-day exchange (shilling) is good.
今朝先令行情蠻好
Kyung-tsau sien-ling 'aung-dzing 'man-hau.

To-day exchange is rising.
今朝先令行情漲者
Kyung-tsau sien-ling 'aung-dzing tsang-tse.

How is exchange (native) to-day?
今朝个釐頭是那能
Kyung-tsau kuh li-deu z na-nung?

Exchange has gone up.
釐頭漲哉 *Li-deu tsang-tse.*

Exchange has gone down.
釐頭跌哉 *Li-deu tih tse.*

Silver is strong to-day.

今朝个銀根寬

Kyung-tsau-kuh nyung-kung khwen.

Silver is weak to-day.

今朝个銀根緊

Kyung-tsau-kuh nyung-kung kyung.

What is your opinion of exchange?

儂个意思釐頭那能

Noong-kuh i-s li-deu na-nung?

I cannot say.

我勿能話 *Ngoo 'veh nung wo.*

I think it will go up.

我想要漲點 *Ngoo siang iau tsang-tien.*

I think it will go down.

双想要跌點 *Ngoo siang iau tih-tien.*

How is business to-day?

今朝个生意那能

Kyung-tsau-kuh sang-i na-nung?

Is your business good?

儂个生意好否 *Noong-kuh sang-i hau va?*

Is there any improvement?

有啥起色否 *Yeu sa chi-suh va?*

No, about the same.

差勿多 *Tsho-'veh-too.*

How is the market?

市面那能 *Z-mien na-nung?*

The market is steady.

市面是穩當个 *Z-mien z 'wung-taung-kuh.*

Prices are high to-day.

今朝个價錢貴哉

Kyung tsau-kuh ka-dien kyui-tse.

Prices are low to-day.

今朝个價錢賤哉

Kyung-tsau-kuh ka-dien jang tse.

The market is much stronger.

市面寬子多化哉

Z-mien khwen-ts too-hau tse.

The market is much weaker.

市面緊子多化哉

Z-mien kyung-ts too-hau tse.

How is the cotton market to-day?

今朝棉花市面那能

Kyung-tsau mien-hwo z-mien na-nung?

This year's tea business is better than last year's.

今年茶葉市面比舊年好點

Kyung-nien dzo-yih z-mien pi jeu-nien hau-tien.

At present trade in foreign goods is not very remunerative.

近來做洋貨生意勿能賺銅錢个

Jung-le tsoo yang-hoo sang-i veh-nung dzan doong-dien-kuh.

Call the compradore.

請賬房 (or 買辦) 來

Tshing tsang-vaung (or *'ma-ban*) *le.*

Call the shroff.

叫收賬个 (or 式老夫) 來

Kyau seu-tsang-kuh (or *seh-lau-fu*) *le.*

Call the coolie.

叫出店 (or 小工) 來

Kyau tsheh-tien (or *siau-koong*) *le.*

Take this letter to the Chinese Post office.

第个信送到郵政局去

Di-kuh sing soong tau Yeu-tsung-jok chi.

British Post Office.

大英書新館 *Da-iung Su-sing-kwen.*

United States Post Office.

花旗書信館 *Hwo-ji Su-sing-kwen.*

German Post Office.

德國書信館 *Tuk-kok Su-sing-kwen.*

French Post Office

法國書信館 *Fah-kok Su-sing-kwen.*

Japanese Post Office.

東洋書信館 *Toong-yang Su-sing-kwen.*

Russian Post Office.

俄國書信館 *Ngoo-kok Su-sing-kwen.*

Just now I am very busy; come again.

現在我忙來死,後首再來

Yien-dze ngoo maung-le-si; 'eu-seu tse le.

Come back to-morrow.

明朝再來 *Ming-tsau tse le.*

Come back this afternoon.

下半日再來 *'Au-pen-nyih tse le.*

Going Up-Country.

Call a native boat.

叫一隻本地船 *Kyau ih-tsak pung-di zen.*

I want to go to the hills.[3]

我要到山上去

Ngoo iau tau San-laung chi.

I want to go to Soochow.

我要到蘇州去

Ngoo iau tau Soo-tseu chi.

I want to go to the Great Lake.

我要到太湖去

Ngoo iau tau Tha-'oo chi.

I want to go to Hangchow.

我要到杭州去

Ngoo iau tau 'Aung-tseu chi.

Laudah, how many men are required for this boat?

老大第隻船上用幾个人

Lau-da, di-tsak zen-laung yoong kyi-kuh nyung?

---

[3] To many Shanghai people "the hills" mean: 茶山 , *Dzo San.*

I require four men.

我必要用四个人

Ngoo pih-iau yoong s-kuh nyung.

What is the total outlay each day for this boat?

第隻船每日要幾化費用

Di-tsak zen 'me-nyih iau kyi-hau fi-yoong?

You must arrange for a tow.

儂要預備拖个小火輪船

Noong iau yui-be thoo-kuh siau hoo-lung-zen.

What is the cost of the tow to Soochow?

到蘇州小火輪个拖錢耍幾化

Tau Soo-tseu siau hoo-lung-zen-kuh thoo-dien iau kyi-hau?

What is the cost of the tow to Hangchow?

到杭州小火輪个拖錢要幾化

Tau 'Aung-tseu siau hoo-lung-zen-kuh thoo-dien iau kyi-hau?

The boat must be made clean.

船要收作來乾淨

Zen iau seu-tsauh-le koen-zing.

When does the tide ebb?

潮水幾時退 (or 落).

Dzau-s kyi-z the (or *lauh*)?

When does the tide flow?

潮水幾時漲 (or 來)

Dzau-s kyi-z tsang (or *le*)?

Now the tide is contrary.

現在是逆水 *Yien-dze z nyuh-s.*

Now the tide is favorable.

現在是順水 *Yien-dze z zung-s.*

To-night the boat must stop here.

今夜船要停拉此地

Kyung-ya zen iau ding la tsh-di.

Shut the windows.

要關窗 *Iau kwan tshaung.*

Open the windows.

要開窗 *Iau khe tshaung.*

Bring some hot water.

拿點熱水來 *Nau tien nyih-s le.*

Bring some cold water.

拿點冷水來 *Nau tien lang-s le.*

We start at one o'clock.

伲要一點鐘開船

Nyi iau ih tien-tsoong khe zen.

We go back to Shanghai.

伲要回到上海去

Nyi iau we tau Zaung-he chi.

You must yulo (scull) more quickly.

搖來快點 *Yau-le khwa-tien.*

Now the wind is favorable.

現在是順風 *Yien-dze z zung-foong.*

Raise the sail. 可以扯蓬 *Khau-i tsha boong.*

Lower the sail. 可以落蓬 *Khau-i lauh boong.*

Tow the boat. 要拖縴 *Iau thoo-chien.*

When will our boat arrive?
伲个船幾時到 *Nyi-kuh zen kyi-z tau?*

Roll up the bedding.
鋪蓋打去來 *Phoo-ke tang-chi-le.*

Call coolies. 叫小工來 *Kyau siau-koong le.*

Call two sedan chairs.
叫兩頂轎子來
Kyau liang-ting jau-ts le.

Take the bedding and luggage to my house.
鋪蓋咾行李送到我个屋裡
Phoo-ke lau 'ang-li soong tau ngoo-kuh ok-li.

Do not forget the things.
物事勿要忘記
Meh-z 'veh iau maung-kyi.

When does the railway train start from Shanghai for Soochow?
火車從上海到蘇州幾點鐘開車
Hoo-tsho dzoong Zaung-he tau Soo-tseu kyi tien-tsoong khe tsho?

In the morning it starts at 8.45;[4] arriving at Soochow at 10.47 a.m.[5]
早晨八點三刻開車,十點三刻過二分到蘇州
Tsau zung pah-tien san-khuh khe tsho, zeh-tien san-khuh koo nyi fung tau Soo-tseu.

---

[4] These times and fares were correct at date of printing; but as alterations are inevitable these must not be taken as a guide.

[5] These times and fares were correct at date of printing; but as alterations are inevitable these must not be taken as a guide.

The first class fare from Shanghai to Soochow is $3.15.[6]

上海到蘇州頭等客位三塊一角五分

Zaung-he tau Soo-tseu deu-tung khak-we san khwe ih kauh ng fung.

The second class is $1.60; the third class is 85 cents.[7]

二等客位一塊六角,三等客位八角五分

Nyi-tung khak-we ih khwe loh kauh; San-tung khak-we pah kauh ng fung.

Each passenger can take .... packages, weighing 60 lbs.[8]

每人可以帶〇件行李,重六十磅

Me nyung khau-i ta .... jien ‘ang-li, dzoong lok-seh paung.

When you come to the station, call a chair to go into the city.

儂到之車站可以叫一頂轎子進城

Noong tau-ts tsho-dzan khau-i kyau ih-ting jau-ts tsing dzung.

[6] These times and fares were correct at date of printing; but as alterations are inevitable these must not be taken as a guide.

[7] These times and fares were correct at date of printing; but as alterations are inevitable these must not be taken as a guide.

[8] These times and fares were correct at date of printing; but as alterations are inevitable these must not be taken as a guide.

The Cook (大司務).

To cook.

燒 *Sau.*

To boil.

煠 or 燉

Zah (or *tung*).

To roast, bake or toast.

烘 *Hoong.*

To fry.

煎

Tsien.

To broil.

燻 or 烤

Hyuin, or *khau* (not much used).

To steam.

蒸

Tsung.

To stew.[9]

燉 or 煱 or 燽

Tung, or *'oo* or *tok.*

[9] No exact term in Shanghai colloquial; cooks in imitation of the English sound say "*S-thoo*" 水拖 .

Boil water for tea.

燉茶 *Tung dzo.*

Make tea (by pouring boiling water on the leaves).

㳮 (or 泡) 茶 *Phau dzo.*

Boiled (*or* boiling) water.

開水 *Khe-s,* 滾水 *Kwung-s.*

Go and buy (literally cook) some hot (boiled) water.

去㳮點開水來

Chi phau tien khe-s le.

Buy some hot water.

買點熱水 *Ma tien nyik-s.*

Buy some hot (*i.e.*, boiled) water (for drinking).

買點開水 *Ma tien khe-s.*

Make chicken soup.

要做雞湯 *Iau tsoo kyi-thaung.*

Make chicken jelly.

要做雞絲凍 *Iau tsoo kyi s-toong.*

Make calves' foot jelly.

要做小牛脚凍

Iau tsoo siau-nyeu kyak-toong.

Go to the market and buy Meat, Fish, Vegetables, Chicken, Hen's Eggs, Pheasant, Ducks, Wild Goose, Goose, Turkey, Snipe, Small Water Duck, Oranges, Pumelo, Apples, Peaches, Apricots, Biboes, Strawberries, Lichees, Pineapple, Grapes, Beans, String Beans, Cabbage, Spinach, Cauliflower, Turnips, Carrots, Shoulder of Mutton, Leg of Mutton, Mutton Chops, Roast Beef, Steak, Bread, Biscuits, Milk, Butter, Tea, Sugar, Coffee, Rice, Flour, Oatmeal, Salt, Matches, Kerosene Oil, Coals,

Charcoal, Firewood.

到街上去買肉,魚,蔬菜,雞,雞蛋,野雞,鴨,野鵝,鵝,火雞,竹雞,小水鴨,橘子,文旦,蘋果,桃子,杏子,枇杷,外國楊梅,荔枝,婆羅蜜,葡萄,荳,刀荳,捲心菜,菠菜,花菜,蘿蔔,紅蘿蔔,羊个前腿 or 後腿,羊个後背,腰窩,燒肉坯,牛肉排,饅頭,餲餅,牛奶,奶油,茶葉,糖,茄菲,米,米粉,大麥粉,鹽,自來火,火油,煤,炭,柴.

Tau ka-laung chi ma nyok, ng, soo-tshe, kyi, kyi-dan, ya-kyi, ah, ya-ngoo, ngoo, hoo-kyi, tsok-kyi, siau-s-ah, kyoeh-ts, vung-tan, bing-koo, dau-ts, 'ang-ts, bih-bo, Nga-kok yang-me, li-ts, poo-loo-mih, beh-dau, deu, tau-deu, kyoen-sing-tshe, poo-tshe, hwo-tshe, Lau-bok, 'oong lau-bok, yang-kuh dzien-the (or *'eu-the yang-kuh 'eu-pe, iau-oo, sau-nyok-phe, nyeu-nyok-ba, men-deu, thah-ping, nyeu-na, na-yeu, dzo-yik, daung, kha-fi, mi, mi-fung, da-mak-fung, yien, z-le-hoo, hoo-yeu, me, than, za.*

Don't use pork fat to fry.

勿要用猪油煎

'Veh iau yoong ts-yeu tsien.

Use beef fat to fry.

要用牛油煎 *Iau yoong nyeu-yeu tsien.*

Is it ready?

好末 or 好哉否

Hau meh (or *hau tse va?*)

Keep this; we can use to-morrow.

要擺拉,明朝再用

Iau pa-la; ming-tsau tse yoong.

This is too salt.

第个忒鹹

Di-kuh thuk 'an.

This is too fresh (has not enough salt).

第个忒淡

Di-kuh thuh dan.

This is under-cooked.

燒來忒生

Sau le thuh sang.

This is cooked too long.

燒來忒熟

Sau le thuh zok.

This needs a hot fire.

要旺火燒 *Iau yaung-hoo sau.*

This wants a slow fire.

要文火燒 *Iau vung-hoo sau.*

Warm this meat.

熱熱第个肉 *Nyih-nyih di-kuh nyok.*

Get it ready presently.

就要燒 *Zieu iau sau.*

Get it ready quickly.

快點燒 *Khwa-tieu sau.*

All meals must be ready on time.

吃飯要有一定个時候

Chuh-van iau yeu ih-ding-kuh z-'eu.

This cooking stove is broken; have it repaired.

鐵灶有毛病要修

Thih-tsau yeu mau-bing; iau sieu.

The flue (or chimney) is choked; have it cleaned.

煙囪塞沒,要通

Ien-tshoong suh-meh, iau thoong.

Black the stove.

鐵灶要刷黑

Thih-tsau iau seh huk.

This is not the stove brush; exchange for another.

第个勿是鐵灶个刷帚,要換別个

Di-kuh 'veh-z thih-tsau-kuh seh-tseu; iau wen bih-kuh.

This brush is broken; buy a new one.

第个刷已經壞脫,要買新个

Di-kuh seh i-kyung wa-theh; iau ma sing-kuh.

I have no black lead.

我勿有黑煤 or 黑鉛

Ngoo 'veh yeu huh-me (or *huh khan*).

This pot leaks; have it mended.

第个壺漏者,要修 (or 要銲)

Di-kuh 'oo leu tse; iau sieu (or *iau 'oen*—solder.)

This pot is cracked and can't be mended.

第个壺迸開,勿能再修

Di-kuh 'oo pang-khe, 'veh nung tse sieu.

I want to buy a new kettle.

我要買一把新个水壺

Ngoo iau ma ih-po sing-kuh s-'oo.

I want to buy a large covered jar.

我要買一个有蓋个缽頭

Ngoo iau ma ih-kuh yeu-ke-kuh peh-deu.

I want to buy a small kong.

我要買一隻小缸

Ngoo iau ma ih-tsak siau-kaung.

Buy a ton of soft coal and half a ton of hard coal.

買一噸煙煤咾半噸白煤

Ma ih-tung ien-me lau pen-tung bak-me.

Buy a basket of charcoal.

買一蔞炭 *Ma ih-leu than.*

Have you bought the firewood?

生火个柴買哉否

Sang-hoo-kuh za ma tse 'va?

[I] want [you] to buy ice.

要買點冰

Iau ma tien ping.

Put this in the ice-box.

第个物事要擺拉冰箱裡

Di-kuh meh-z iau pa la ping-siang li.

[I want you to] clean out the ice-box.

冰箱要弄乾淨

Ping-siang iau loong koen-zing.

The ice-box is leaking; have it mended.

冰箱有漏,要修好

Ping-siang yeu leu; iau sieu-hau.

Bring some boiling water.

担滾水 (or 開水)來

Tan kwung-s (or *khe-s le.*)

Make a bowl of arrowroot.

冲一碗藕粉來

Tsoong ih-'wen ngeu-fung le.

Make it thicker than yesterday.

要比昨日厚點

Iau pi zauh-nyih ‘eu-tien.

I am going out; you look after the house.

我要出去,儂要當心房子

Ngoo iau tsheh-chi; noong iau taung-sing vaung-ts.

A friend has asked me to go out to dinner; you don’t need to prepare.

有朋友請我吃夜飯,儂勿要預備哉

Yeu bang-yeu tshing ngoo chuh ya-van; noong ’veh iau yui-be tse.

To-day get supper ready half an hour earlier.

今朝夜飯要早半點鐘

Kyung-tsau ya-van iau tsau pe-tien-tsoong.

Call me at 6 o’clock to-morrow morning.

明朝早晨六點鐘要叫我

Ming-tsau tsau-zung lok tien-tsoong iau kyau ngoo.

Go to the market early to-morrow morning.

明朝要早點到街上去

Ming-tsau iau tsau-tien tau ka-laung chi.

I want to take the accounts now.

現在要算賬

Yien-dze iau soen-tsang.

Your account is all right.

儂个賬勿錯 or 對个

Noong-kuh tsang ’veh tsho (or *te kuh*).

Your account has a mistake.

儂个賬勿對 or 有錯

Noong-kuh tsang ’veh te (or *yeu tsho*).

Your account is more than mine.

儂个賬比我多

Noong-kuh tsang pi ngoo too.

Your account is less than mine.

儂个賬此我少

Noong-kuh tsang pi ngoo sau.

I have already paid this.

第个賬我已經付拉哉

Di-kuh tsang ngoo i-kyung foo-la-tse.

I will pay you to-morrow.

明朝付儂

Ming-tsau foo noong.

Next week I will pay you.

下禮拜付儂

'Au li-pa foo noong.

House Boy (西崽) *and Coolie* (出點).

Light the lamp.

要點燈 *Iau tien tung.*

Call the cook.

呌大司務來 *Kyau da-s-voo le.*

Call the coolie.

呌出店來 (or 苦力)

Kyau tsheh-tien le (or *Khoo-lih*).

(小工 *Siau koong* is frequently used for "coolie," especially for coolie for outside work).

Call a ricksha.

呌一部東洋車來

Kyau ih-boo toong-yang-tsho le.

Set the table.

要擺檯子 (or 要預備檯子)

Iau ba de-ts (or *Iau yui-be de-ts*).

There are guests coming to-day for tiffin.

今朝有客人來吃中飯

Kyung-tsau yeu khak-nyung le chuh tsoong van.

To-day four guests come to dinner (evening meal).

今朝有四个客人來吃夜飯

Kyung-tsau yeu s-kuh khak-nyung le chuh ya-van.

Call an extra boy to help [you.]

要另外叫一个西崽來相帮

Iau ling-nga kyau ih-kuh si-tse le siang-paung.

Clean this room.

第間房子要收作乾淨

Di-kan vaung-ts iau seu-tsauh koen-zing.

Wash this floor.

第个地板要淨

Di-kuh di-pan iau zing.

Sweep this floor.

第个地板要掃

Di-kuh di-pan iau sau.

The door, windows, and base-board of this room I want you to wash.

第間房子裡个門窗咾跌脚板全要淨

Di-kan vaung-ts li-kuh mung, tshaung, lau tih-kyak-pan zen iau zing.

This is not clean; do it again.

第頭勿曾乾淨,要再做

Di-deu 'veh-zung koen-zing, iau tse tsoo.

Use soap and brush it.

要用肥皂來刷

Iau yoong bi-zau le seh.

Don't use a brush here.

第頭勿要用板刷

Di-deu 'veh iau yoong pan-seh.

You must scour the table.

檯子要擦

De-ts iau tshah.

Wipe the table.

檯子要揩

De-ts iau kha.

Bring a feather brush.

担雞毛撢帚來

Tan kyi-mau-toen-tseu le.

Dust the pictures.

畫圖要撢乾淨

Wo-doo iau toen koen-zing.

Use a cloth to dust the room.

第間房子要用布揩乾淨

Di-kan vaung-ts iau yoong poo kha koen-zing.

This cloth is dirty; you must wash it.

第个揩布齷齪,要淨

Di-kuh kha-poo auh-tshauh, iau zing.

Dust (or clean) all things in this room.

第間房子裡个物事,全要揩乾淨

Di-kan vaung-ts-li kuh meh-z, zen iau kha koen-zing.

Clean the windows.

玻璃窗要揩乾淨

Poo-li-tshaung iau kha koen-zing.

These curtains are dirty, change to clean ones.

第个窗帘齷齪,要換乾淨个

Di-kuh tshaung-lien auh-tshauh, iau wen koen-zing-kuh.

Brush this table cover.

第个檯布要刷

Di-kuh de-poo iau seh.

Put these books in order.

第个書要擺好

Di-kuh su iau pa-hau.

Put these things in their proper place.

各様物事,要擺拉應該个地方

Kauh-yang meh-z iau pa la iung-ke-kuh di-faung.

Please come and help me.

請儂來相帮我

Tshing noong le siang-paung ngoo.

This box (trunk) I want taken over there.

第隻箱子要搬到伊頭去

Di-tsah siang-ts iau-pen tau i-deu chi.

Where are you?

儂拉那裡

Noong la 'a-li?

If you want to go out, first tell me.

儂要出去,先告訴我

Noong iau tsheh-chi, sien kau-soo ngoo.

Why are you so idle?

爲啥實蓋懶惰 *We-sa zeh-ke lan-doo?*

At the end of the month you can go.

做到月底儂可以停 (or 可以去)

Tsoo tau nyoeh-ti, noong khau-i ding (or *khau-i chi*).

If you go home, you must get me a substitute.

若是儂歸去,要叫替工

Zak-z noong kyiu-chi, iau kyau thi-koong.

[We] want to use another boy.

再要用一个西崽

Tse iau yoong ih-kuh si-tse.

Can you get me a coolie?

儂可以尋 (or 叫)一个苦力否

Noong khau-i zing (or *kyau*) *ih-kuh khoo-lih va?*

If you want to go (stop work) you must wait till the end of the month.

若是儂要停,要做到月底

Zak-z noong iau ding, iau tsoo tau nyoeh-ti.

[If] you want to go (*or* stop work), you must wait till I find new man.

儂要停,等我尋著新个人

Noong iau ding, tung ngoo zing-dzak sing-kuh nyung.

If you go now it is not convenient to pay your wages.

現在停,勿便付儂工錢

Yien-dze ding, 'veh bien foo noong koong-dien.

[I] will pay at the end of the month.

到月底咾付儂

Tau nyoeh-ti lau foo noong.

[If you] go now I will cut your wages.

現在停,我要齧儂工錢

Yien-dze ding, ngoo iau ngah noong koong-dien.

This cook is not a very good one.

第个大司務勿大好

Di-kuh da-s-voo 'veh da hau.

This coolie is also very lazy.

第个苦力也是懶惰

Di-kuh khoo-lih ‘a-z lan-doo.

I want to put up the stove for this room at once.

第間个火爐就裝起來

Di-kan kuh hoo-loo zieu tsaung-chi-le.

You must first brush it.

先要刷乾淨

Sien iau seh-koen-zing.

Brush these shoes.

第雙鞋子要刷

Di-saung ‘a-ts iau seh.

Brush these clothes and hang in the sun.

衣裳刷之咾晒拉日頭裡

I-zaung seh-ts lau so la nyih-deu li.

Be careful the wind does not blow them away.

當心勿要撥風吹脫

Taung-sing ’veh iau peh foong ths-theh.

Take this out and shake it [clean].

担出去抖抖乾淨

Tan tsheh-chi teu-teu koen-zing.

Open this bundle.

第个包要解開 *Di-kuh pau iau ka-khe.*

Wrap it up.

要包起來 *Iau pau-chi-le.*

Use a rope to tie this.

用繩梱起來

Yoong zung khwung-chi-le.

Buy some strong rope.

要買牢个繩

Iau ma lau-kuh zung.

Buy a basket (with string net on top).

買一隻網籃

Ma ih-tsak maung-lan.

Put all the food into this basket.

吃个物事全擺拉第隻籃裡

Chuh-kuh meh-z zen pa-la di-tsak lan-li.

Buy me a foot-stove and some charcoal (balls).

買一隻脚爐咾幾个炭團

Ma ih-tsak kyak-loo lau kyi-kuh than-doen.

Roll up my bedding.

舖蓋打起來

Phoo-ke tang-chi-le.

Take this letter to...........

第封信送到 ....

Di-foong sing soong tau.........

An answer is wanted.

要回信个

Iau we-sing kuh.

Go to the Chinese Imperial Post Office.

到郵政局去

Tau Yeu-tsung-jok chi.

Go to the Post Office for the mail.

到書信舘去担信來

Tau su-sing-kwen chi tan sing le.

Take this parcel to the Post Office.

第个包送到書信舘去

Di-kuh pau, soong tau su-sing-kwen chi.

Call a wheelbarrow and take these things to the steamer.

呌小車送第个物事到船上去

Kyau siau-tsho soong di-kuh meh-z tau zen laung chi.

Put camphor with the clothes.

衣裳裡要放樟腦

I-zaung-li iau faung tsaung-nau.

The answer says there are two books; why is there only one here?

回信話有兩本書,現在只有一本,啥緣故

We-sing wo yeu liang-pung su; yien-dze tsuh-yeu ih-pung, sa yoen-koo?

The chit book says there is an answer; where is it?

送信簿上寫明有回信,拉那裡

Soong-sing-boo laung sia-ming yeu we-sing, la 'a-li?

This letter is not mine; have you any other?

第封信勿是我个,還有別个否

Di-fong sing 'veh-z ngoo-kuh; wan yeu bih-kuh va?

This is for the next house.

第个物事是隔壁人家个.

Di-kuh meh-z z kah-pih nyung-ka-kuh.

Call a man to put a new cover on this chair.

第隻椅子呌人來換新个椅布

Di-tsak iui-ts, kyau nyung le wen sing-kuh iui poo.

Get a new glass for this broken window.

窗上个碎玻璃要配新个

Tshaung-laung-kuh se poo-li iau phe sing-kuh.

Take this pass-book to the store and bring the things.

担第本簿子到店裏去,拿物事來

Tan di-pung boo-ts tau tien-li chi, nau meh-z le.

Go and buy some bread tickets.

去買饅頭票子來

Chi ma men-deu phiau-ts le.

Take these tickets and exchange for bread.

担第个票子去換饅頭

Tan di-kuh phiau-ts chi wen men-deu.

Go and buy biscuits.

去買點餅乾來

Chi ma tien ping-koen le.

I want a ricksha to go to the French Concession.

要一部東洋車到法租界去

Iau ih-boo toong-yang-tsho tau Fah-tsoo-ka chi.

I want a carriage for half a day.

我要一部馬車用半日

Ngoo iau ih-boo mo-tsho yoong pen-nyih.

I want it again to-morrow.

明朝我再要

Ming-tsau ngoo tse iau.

He asks too much money.

伊討个價錢忒大

Yi thau-kuh ka-dien thuh doo.

Three Dollars are enough.

三塊洋錢彀者

San-khwe yang-dien keu-tse.

This carriage is not good; get another.

第部馬車勿好,要換好个

Di-boo mo-tsho 'veh-hau; iau wen hau-kuh.

I am not very well to-day (*or* am ill).

今朝我勿大爽快 (or 有毛病)

Kyung-tsau ngoo 'veh da saung-khwa (or *yeu mau-bing*).

What is the matter?

啥个毛病 *Sa-kuh mau-bing?*

I don't know what it is.

我勿曉得是啥毛病

Ngoo 'veh hyau-tuh z sa mau-bing.

I've got fever and ague.

我有瘧子 (or 瘧疾)

Ngoo yeu ngauh-ts (or *nyak-dzih*).

I've got fever.

我有寒熱 *Ngoo yeu 'oen-nyih.*

I'll give you a dose of medicine.

我撥儂點藥

Ngoo peh noong tien yak.

You had better see the doctor.

儂要請醫生生看

Noong iau tshing i-sang khoen.

I must go to the hospital.

我要住拉醫院裡

Ngoo iau dzu-la i-yoen-li.

I want to go home.

我要歸去 or 到屋裡去

Ngoo iau kyui-chi (or *tau ok-li chi*).

You can return home for a short time.

儂暫時可以歸去

Noong dzan-z khau-i kyui-chi.

You are still not fit for work.

儂現在還勿能做生活

Noong yien-dze wan 'veh nung tsoo sang-weh.

Come again when you are stronger.

儂好點咾再來

Noong hau-tien lau tse le.

Cook is sick and can't get up.

大司務拉生病,勿能起來

Da-s-voo la sang-bing, 'veh-nung chi-le.

Why do you work so very slowly?

儂做生活爲啥慢來死

Noong tsoo sang-weh we-sa man-le-si?

Because I am tired.

爲之我弛陀

We-ts ngoo sa-doo.

Perhaps you go out too much at night.

恐怕儂夜頭出去忒多

Khoong-pho noong ya-deu tsheh-chi thuh too.

I think you smoke opium (*or* drink wine.)

我想儂吃雅片煙 (or 吃酒)

Ngoo siang noong chuh ia-phien-ien (or *chuh tsieu*).

Your clothes and hat are untidy.

儂个衣帽勿整齊

Noong-kuh i-mau 'veh tsung-zi.

Don't have your shoes down at the heel.

儂勿要拖鞋皮

Noong 'veh iau thoo 'a-bi.

Have you not combed your hair to-day?

儂今朝勿曾梳頭否

Noong kyung-tsau 'veh-zung s-deu va?

This is not proper (respectful.)

第个是無規矩个

Di-kuh z m kwe-kyui-kuh.

Call amah to come.

叫阿媽來

Kyau A-ma le.

Amah (阿媽).

Take baby out.

領小囝到外頭去

Ling siau-noen tau nga-deu chi.

Go to the Gardens.

領小囝到花園裡去

Ling siau-noen tau hwo-yoen-li chi.

If it is too cold, come home.

若是忒冷,就轉來

Zak-z thuh lang, zieu tsen-le.

Don't sit in the wind.

勿要坐拉風裡

'Veh iau zoo la foong-li.

Don't get in the sun.

勿要到日頭裡去

'Veh iau tau nyih-deu-li chi.

Baby's clothes you can wash.

小囝个衣裳要儂淨

Siau-noen-kuh i-zaung iau noong zing.

[You can] also iron them.

也要湯

'A iau thaung.

This you can give to the washerman.

第个可以撥汏衣裳个人淨

Di-kuh khau-i peh da-i-zaung-kuh nyung zing.

Use hot water to wash flannel.

呿囒絨用熱水淨

Fah-lan-nyoong yoong nyih-s zing.

This water is too cold.

第个水忒冷

Di-kuh s thuh lang.

Wring dry.

要絞來乾點

Iau kau le koen tien.

Hang them up (as on a line to dry or air).

要晾起來

Iau laung-chi-le.

Shake well and hang up in the sun.

要抖抖咾晒拉日頭裏

Iau teu-teu lau so la nyih-deu-li.

[When] ironing clothes, do not have them too dry.

衣裳要湯,勿要忒乾

I-zaung iau thaung, 'veh iau thuh koen.

Mend this.

第个要補 *Di-kuh iau poo.*

Mend these stockings.

第雙襪要補

Di-saung mah iau poo.

[I] want you to knit stockings.

要儂結一雙襪

Iau noong kyih ih-saung mah.

I want you to sew this.

我要儂做 (or 縫) 第个

Ngoo iau noong tsoo (or *voong*) *di-kuh.*

I cannot sew.

我縫勿來个

Ngoo voong-'veh-le-kuh.

Then you must learn.

蓋末儂要學

Keh-meh noong iau 'auh.

My children are not very small; so, therefore, I want you to sew and knit and help me (*lit.*, help in hand work).

我个小囝勿算頂小，所以要儂相帮我做手裡生活

Ngoo-kuh siau-noen 'veh soen ting siau, soo-i iau noong siang-paung ngoo tsoo seu-li sang-weh.

Put on (baby's) outdoor clothes and take him out.

著之外罩衣裳咾領伊到外頭去

Tsak-ts nga-tsau-i-zaung lau ling yi tau nga-deu chi.

Don't buy anything and give her to eat.

勿要買啥物事撥伊吃

'Veh iau ma sa meh-z peh yi chuh.

Don't give him anything to eat unless I say so.

若是我勿告訴儂末，儂勿要撥啥伊吃

Zak-z ngoo 'veh kau-soo noong meh, noong 'veh iau peh sa yi chuh.

Because she is sick she cannot eat this.

爲之伊有毛病，所以勿能吃第个

We-ts yi yeu mau-bing, soo-i 'veh nung chuh di-kuh.

My wages are too small, please increase them.

我个工錢勿彀，請儂加點

Ngoo-kuh koong-dien 'veh keu, tshing noong ka-tien.

Just now I cannot increase; afterwards I will give you more.

現在我勿能加，後首咾加儂

Yien-dze ngoo 'veh nung ka, 'eu-seu lau ka noong.

If you cannot give more now, I must leave you.

若是儂現在勿能加，我只得停 (or 離開儂)

Zah-z noong yien-dze 'veh nung ka, ngoo tsuh-tuh ding (or *li-khe noong*).

Beginning with next month I promise to increase one dollar; next year I will again raise you one dollar.

下个月起頭我應許加儂一塊，到開年我再加儂一塊

'Au-kuh-nyoeh chi-deu ngoo iung-hyui ka noong ih-khwe, tau khe-nien ngoo tse ka noong ih-khwe.

The Gentlemen's Tailor (裁縫).

Tailor	裁縫	*Ze-voong.*
Jacket	馬褂	*Mo-kwo.*
Vest	背心	*Pe-sing.*
Overcoat	大衣 (or 外罩衣)	*Doo-i* (or *Nga tsau-i.*)
Trousers	褲子	*Khoo-ts.*
Tie	結子	*Kyih-ts.*
Collar	領頭	*Ling-deu.*
Stockings	襪	*Mah.*
Singlet	襯衫	*Tshung-san.*

[For morning coat, and such articles of apparel as are not used by the Chinese, there is no proper Chinese equivalent.]

I want you to make a suit of clothes.

我要儂做一套衣裳

Ngoo iau noong tsoo ih-thau i-zaung.

Make me a pair of trousers.

做一條褲子

Tsoo ih-diau khoo-ts.

Have you got your patterns with you?

儂有樣子否

Noong yeu yang-ts va?

Can you recommend this cloth?

儂想第个布好用否

Noong siang di-kuh poo hau-yoong va?

This colour is too dark;

第个顔色忒黑

Di-kuh ngan-suh thuh huh.

I want a lighter cloth for summer wear.

我要薄點个布,爲之夏天咾用

Ngoo iau bok-tien kuh poo, we-ts ‘au-thien lau yoong.

What will the cost be?

啥價錢

Sa ka-dien?

I want a good fit.

我要儂做來配身 (or 合式个)

Ngoo iau noong tsoo-le phe-sung (or *’eh-suh kuh.*)

The lining must be good.

夾裡要用好个料作

Kah-li iau yoong hau-kuh liau-tsok.

How long will it take to finish? [How much labour is there?]

要幾化工夫

Iau kyi-hau koong-foo?

When will it be ready to try on?

幾時可以拿來試試看 (or 演演看)

Kyi-z khau-i nau-le s-s-khoen (or *ien-ien-khoen*).

The sleeves are too long.

袖子忒長 *Zieu-ts thuh dzang.*

The legs are too short.

褲脚忒短 *Khoo-kyak thuh toen.*

This jacket does not fit.

第个馬褂勿配身

Di-kuh mo-kwo 'veh phe-sung.

This overcoat is tight across the shoulders.

第件大衣个肩膀忒緊

Di-jien doo-i kuh kyien-paung thuh kyung.

The vest is too loose across the chest.

背心个胸膛忒寬

Pe-sing kuh hyoong-daung thuh-khwen.

The collar is too high.

領頭忒高 *Ling-deu thuh kau.*

I want a pocket inside.

裡向也要有袋

Li-hyang 'a iau yeu de.

The trousers must have side pockets.

褲子兩傍應該有袋

Khoo-ts liang-baung iung-ke yeu de.

I want you to mend these trousers.

第條褲子要儂修

Di diau khoo-ts iau noong sieu.

Put more buttons on.

鈕子要多點

Nyeu-ts iau too-tien.

Put new cuffs on these shirts.

汗衫上要換新个袖頭

'Oen-san-laung iau wen sing-kuh zieu-deu.

[This] shirt front is frayed; I want a new one.

汗衫个前面壞者,要換新个

'Oen-san kuh zien-mien wa-tse, iau wen sing-kuh.

The material is mine, how much for making only?

料作我自辦,不過做工要幾錢

Liau-tsauk ngoo z-ban, peh-koo tsoo-koong iau kyi-dien?

The Ladies' Tailor.

Call a tailor.

叫一个裁縫來

Kyau ih-kuh ze-voong le.

I want you to make a dress.

我要儂做一套衣裳[10]

Ngoo iau noong tsoo ih-thau i-zaung.[11]

I want you to make a skirt.

我要儂做一條裙

Ngoo iau noong tsoo ih-diau juin.

I want you to make a bodice.

我要儂做一个肚兜

Ngoo iau noong tsoo ih-kuh doo-teu.

I want you to make a jacket.

我要儂做一件馬褂

Ngoo iau noong tsoo ih-jien mo-kwo.

I want you to make a cloak.

我要儂做一件外罩个袍褂

Ngoo iau noong tsoo ih-jien nga-tsau-kuh bau-kwo.

---

[10] This is the same expression that is used for a suit of clothes.
[11] This is the same expression that is used for a suit of clothes.

This sleeve is too long; make it shorter.

第个袖子忒長;要做來短點

Di-kuh zieu-ts thuh dzang; iau tsoo-le toen-tien.

This garment is too tight; make it easier.

第件衣裳身胚忒緊,要做來寬點

Di-jien i-zaung sung-phe thuh kyung; iau tsoo-le khwen tien.

This is too wide (or loose); make tighter.

第件衣裳身胚忒寬,要做來緊點

Di-jien i-zaung sung-phe thuh khwen; iau tsoo-le kyung tien.

Make like this pattern.

照第个樣式咾做

Tsau di-kuh yang-suh lau tsoo.

Please bring me samples of native cloth (to let me see).

請儂擔點本地布个樣子撥我看看

Tshing noong tan tien pung-di poo-kuh yang-ts, peh-ngoo khoen-khoen.

Please bring me samples of foreign cloth (to let me see).

請儂擔點外國布个樣子撥我看看

Tshing noong tan tien nga-kok poo-kuh yang-ts, peh ngoo khoen-khoen.

Have you samples of grass cloth?

儂有夏布个樣子否

Noong yeu 'au-poo kuh yang-ts va?

What you have of broad and narrow cloth, bring and let me see.

所有闊咾狹个布,全擔來讓我看看

Soo yeu khweh lau 'ah kuh poo, zen tan-le nyang ngoo khoen-khoen.

When can you finish it?

幾時可以做好 (or 做得好)

Kyi-z khau-i tsoo-hau? (or *tsoo-tuh-hau*).

I want you to do it quicker.

我要儂快點做

Ngoo iau noong khwa-tien tsoo.

Can you finish it this week?

拉第个禮拜裏,做得好否

La di-kuh li-pa li, tsoo-tuh hau va?

This week it is impossible to finish.

拉第个禮拜裏,來勿及做好

La di-kuh li-pa li, le-'veh-ji tsoo-hau.

Then next week certainly must finish.

蓋末下个禮拜,一定要做好

Keh-meh 'au-kuh li-pa, ih-ding iau tsoo-hau.

How much will it cost to make these clothes?

第件衣裳做工啥價錢

Di-jien i-zaung tsoo-koong sa ka-dien?

You ask too big a price.

儂討个價錢忒貴.

Noong thau-kuh ka-dien thuh kyui.

Yes (*or* all right), I can pay you this price.

好个,我可以撥儂第个價錢

Hau-kuh, ngoo khau-i peh noong di-kuh ka-dieh.

Why have you not done as I told you?

爲啥勿照我告訴儂个樣子咾做

We-sa 'veh tsau ngoo kau-soo noong-kuh yang-ts lau tsoo?

You have done very well. When I have more work I shall want you to do it (*lit.*, and another time I will want you to do work.)

儂做來蠻好,下回我還要儂做

Noong tsoo-le 'man-hau; 'au-we ngoo wan iau noong tsoo.

The Washerman (淨衣裳个人).

Take these clothes and wash them.

第个衣裳擔去淨 (or 汏)

Di-kuh i-zaung tan-chi zing (or *da*).

Be careful in washing this; and do not tear it.

要當心淨;勿要淨破

Iau taung-sing zing; 'veh iau zing-phoo.

This garment wants starch, but do not make it too stiff.

第件衣裳要用點漿,但是勿要忒硬

Di-jien i-zaung iau yoong tien tsiang, dan-z 'veh iau thuh ngang.

Do not starch this garment.

第件衣裳勿要漿

Di-jien i-zaung, 'veh iau tsiang.

See, you have torn this garment.

諾,看看,第件衣裳撥儂弄壞者

Nau! khoen-khoen! di-jien i-zaung peh noong loong-wa-tse.

See, this window curtain has been spoiled by you.

儂看,第个窗帘撥儂弄壞者

Noong khoen, di-kuh tshaung-lien peh noong loong-wa-tse.

It is dirty, wash again.

弄齷齪者，要再淨

Loong auh tshauh tse; iau tse zing.

One piece is still missing, why?

還缺少一件，啥緣故

Wan choeh-sau ih-jien; sa yoen-koo?

It is lost; I will try to find it.

失脫者，我再要尋尋看

Seh-theh tse; ngoo tse iau zing-zing-khoen.

If you cannot find it, you must pay for it.

若是尋勿著，要儂賠个

Zah-z zing-'veh-dzak, iau noong be kuh.

What is the price for washing one piece?

淨一件啥價錢

Zing ih-jien sa ka-dien?

Three cents a piece.

三分洋錢一件

San-fung yang-dien i-jien.

Bring these clothes back in two or three days.

第件衣裳兩三日就要擔來

Di-jien i-zaung liang san nyih zieu iau tan-le.

I am going away (*or* leaving Shanghai) presently.

我就要出門 (or 我就要離開上海)

Ngoo zieu iau tsheh-mung (or *ngoo zieu iau li-khe Zaung-he*).

So you must bring back my clothes at once.

所以我个衣裳就擔來

Soo-i ngoo-kuh i-zaung zieu tan-le.

These clothes are not ironed properly; iron them again.

第件衣裳燙來勿好,要再燙

Di-jien i-zaung thaung-le 'veh hau; iau tse thaung.

These clothes are not washed properly, wash them again.

第件衣裳淨來勿乾淨,要再淨

Di-jien i-zaung zing le 'veh koen-zing, iau tse zing.

Don't put any soda in the water.

水裡勿要放鹻

S-li 'veh iau faung kan.

As it easily takes out the colour.

爲之容易退顏色

We-ts yoong-yi the ngan-suh.

How many pieces have you washed this month?

第个月裡淨之幾件衣裳

Di-kuh nyoeh-li zing-ts kyi-jien i-zaung?

The Mafoo (馬夫).

I. Riding.

Saddle the horse.

裝好馬

Tsaung-hau mo.

The girths are too loose.

馬肚帶忒寬

Mo-doo-ta thuh khwen.

Tighten up the girths.

馬肚帶要收緊

Mo-doo-ta iau seu kyung.

Lengthen (or lower) the stirrup.

馬踏櫈要放下點

Mo-dah-tung iau faung 'au-tien.

Those stirrup irons are not bright (or not clean).

馬踏櫈个鐵擦來勿亮 or 勿乾淨

Mo-dah-tung-kuh thih tshah le 'veh liang (or *veh koen-zing*).

Loosen the curb (chain.)

馬嚼鐵放寬點

Mo-ziak-thih faung khwen tien.

Have you put on the saddle-cloth?

馬鞍子个布櫬拉末

Mo-oen-ts-kuh-poo tshung la meh?

Don't take off the rug.

毯子勿要擔脫

Than-ts veh iau tan-theh.

Take off the rug.

毯子要擔去

Than-ts iau tan-chi.

When did you feed the pony?

儂幾時喂个馬料

Noong kyi-z iui-kuh mo-liau?

Give him a good feed.

要撥好个馬料伊吃

Iau peh hau-kuh mo-liau yi chuh.

Has he had a drink?

有吃過水否

Yeu chuh-koo s va?

That saddle does not fit properly.

馬鞍子裝來勿好 (or 勿妥帖)

Mo-oen-ts tsaung le 'veh hau (or *veh thoo thih*).

Walk him round a bit.

牽之讓伊走走

Chien-ts nyang yi tseu-tseu.

Don't feed him now.

現在勿要撥啥伊吃

Yien-dze 'veh iau peh sa yi chuh.

He is very hot.

伊是頂熱 (or 伊是熱得極拉)

Yi z ting nyih (or *Yi z nyih tuh-juh la*).

Don't give him any water.

勿要撥水伊吃

'Veh iau peh s yi chuh.

That pony is sick.

伊隻馬有病

I-tsak mo yeu bing.

Go and get the veterinary surgeon.

去喊馬醫來

Chi lian mo-i le.

Hold him until I get on.

儂牽牢拉讓我騎上去

Noong chien-lau-la, nyang ngoo ji-zaung-chi.

Put more straw in his stall (or box.)

馬棚裏多放點稻柴

Mo-bang-li too faung tien dau-za.

The pony is very dirty; give him a good rub-down.

馬齷齪來;要刷乾淨

Mo auh-thsauh le; iau seh koen-zing.

II. Driving.

Get the carriage ready.

馬車裝起來

Mo-tsho tsaung-chi-le.

Bring the carriage round.
馬車牽過來
Mo-tsho chien-koo-le.

The carriage is not clean.
馬車勿乾淨
Mo-tsho 'veh koen-zing.

The lamps are dirty.
燈是齷齪个
Tung z auh-tshauh kuh.

Are there candles in the lamps?
燈裡有蠟燭否
Tung-li yeu lah-tsok va?

The collar doesn't fit.
軛頭裝來勿伏帖
Ah-deu tsaung le veh vok-thih.

It will hurt the horse's shoulder.
要擦傷馬頸骨个
Iau tshah-saung mo-kyung-kweh-kuh.

Keep the harness clean and in good order.
馬傢生要乾淨咾合式个
Mo ka-sang iau koen-zing lau 'eh-suh kuh.

Don't go (drive) too quickly.
勿要忒快
'Veh iau thuh khwa.

(Drive) more quickly.
要快點
Iau khwa-tien.

Stay here until I come back.

停拉此地等我轉來

Ding la tsh-di, tung ngoo tsen-le.

At ten o'clock come back.

十點鐘再來

Zeh tien-tsoong tse le.

I want the carriage at nine o'clock.

九點鐘我要馬車

Kyeu tien-tsoong ngoo iau mo-tsho.

(Those) wheels are loose.

輪盤鬆者

Lung-ben soong tse.

Put new washers on.

要換新个拈墊

Iau wen sing-kuh nyien-dien.

I want a two-horse carriage.

我要雙馬車

Ngoo iau saung mo-tsho.

Be careful with that horse.

當心伊隻馬

Taung-sing i-tsak mo.

He may run away.

伊要逃走 or 跑開

Yi iau dau-tseu (or *bau-khe.*)

Purchasing.

I want to buy china.

我要買磁器

Ngoo iau ma dz-chi.

Silk.

絲綢

S-dzeu.

Embroidery.

顧繡

Koo-sieu.

Furs.

皮貨

Bi-hoo.

Old curios.

古董

Koo-toong.

Cloisonné ware.

珐藍个物事

Fah-lan kuh meh-z.

A blue bowl with cover.

淡描蓋碗

Dan-miau ke-'wen.

Knife cash.

刀錢

Tau-dzien.

Ancient cash.

古錢

Koo-dzien.

Wood Carvings.

木刻玩器

Mok-khuh wan-chi.

Carvings.

刻作

Khuh-tsauh.

Silver ware.

銀器

Nyung-chi.

Boxes of puzzles.

七巧板

Tshih-chau-pan.

Teapots.

茶壺

Dzo-'oo.

An incense burner.

香爐

Hyang-loo.

Please show me your wares.

儂个貨色請儂撥我看看

Noong-kuh hoo-suh tshing noong peh ngoo khoen-khoen.

What is the price of this?

第个啥價錢

Di-kuh sa ka-dien?

This is too dear.

第个價錢忒貴

Di-kuh ka-dien thuh kyui.

Can you make it cheaper?

可以賤點否

Khau-i jang-tien va?

This is imitation.

第个是翻做个

Di-kuh z fan-tsoo-kuh.

This is not real.

第个勿是眞个

Di-kuh 'veh-z tsung-kuh.

Can you use these dollars?

第个洋錢好用否

Di-kuh yang-dien hau yoong va?

What discount on Hongkong dollars?

每塊香港洋錢鬶脫幾化

'Me-khwe Hyang-kaung yang-dien ngah-theh kyi-hau?

What is the value of Japanese yen?

每塊日本洋錢申幾化

Me-khwe Zeh-pung yang-dien sung kyi-hau?

How many Mexican dollars will an English sovereign bring?

每磅金洋値英洋幾化

Me paung kyung-yang dzuk Iung-yang kyi-hau?

What is the value of American dollars?

每塊花旗洋錢値幾化

'Me khwe Hwo-ji yang-dien dzuh kyi-hau?

The Chinese Teacher (先生).

I want a (Chinese) teacher.

我要請一位先生

Ngoo iau tshing ih-we sien-sang.

I want to learn Mandarin.

我要學官話

Ngoo iau 'auh Kwen-wo.

I want to learn the Shanghai dialect.

我要學上海土白

Ngoo iau 'auh Zaung-he thoo-bak.

Good morning, teacher.

先生早呀

Sien-sang tsau 'a.

My Chinese words are few.

我个中國說話勿多

Ngoo-kuh Tsoong-kok seh-wo 'veh-too.

I want to study in the morning.

我要拉早晨讀書

Ngoo iau la tsau-zung dok-su.

What hour in the morning to begin?

早晨幾點鐘起頭

Tsau-zung kyi tien-tsoong chi-deu?

From seven to eight o'clock.

七點鐘到八點鐘

Tshih tien-tsoong tau pah tien-tsoong.

Can you come earlier?

儂能彀早點來否

Noong nung-keu tsau-tien le va?

What hour is most convenient?

啥時候頂便當

Sa z-'eu ting bien-taung.

How much a month do you wish?

每月儂要幾化薪水

'Me nyoeh noong iau kyi-kau sing-soe?

If each day [we] study one hour [I] want eight dollars.

若是每日讀一點鐘要八塊洋錢

Zak-z 'me nyih dok ih tien-tsoong iau pah-khwe yang-dien.

What book do you think I should study?

儂想讀啥个書

Noong siang dok sa-kuh su?

To aspirate is important.

出風是要緊个

Tsheh-foong z iau-kyung kuh.

Read it over again.

再讀一遍

Tse dok ih-pien.

[To teacher] Should I learn to write the characters?

儂想我要學寫中國字否

Noong siang ngoo iau 'auh sia Tsoong-kok z va?

[To teacher] Do I speak correctly?

我話來對否

Ngoo wo le te va?

[To student] You do not speak distinctly.

儂話來勿淸爽

Noong wo le 'veh tshing-saung.

Speak more quickly.

話來快點 *Wo-le khwa-tien.*

Speak more slowly.

話來慢點 *Wo-le man-tien.*

You speak too quick.

儂話來忒決

Noong wo le thuh-khwa.

To listen to other people's idiom is important.

聽別人个話法是要緊个

Thing bih-nyung-kuh wo-fah z iau-kyung-kuh.

[We have] finished the study of this book; may [we] study Yates' Lessons?[12]

第本書讀完之,可以讀中國譯語妙法否

Di pung su dok-wen-ts, khau-i dok Tsoong-kok Yuk Nyui Miau Fah va?

Sir, please write a letter for me.

先生請儂替我寫一封信

Sien-sang, tshing noong thi ngoo sia ih foong sing.

[12] Since writing these Sentences new Lessons on the Shanghai Dialect have been prepared by Rev. L. Hawks Pott, D.D.(卜先生).

[To teacher] To-morrow I have matters [to attend to] and will not be able to study.

明朝我有事體,勿能讀書

Ming-tsau ngoo yeu z-thi, 'veh nung dok-su.

[To student] The day after to-morrow I go from home and cannot come to teach.

後日我要出門,勿能來教書

'Eu-nyih ngoo iau tsheh-mung, 'veh nung le kau su.

At the beginning, of next week I want to go to the hills for a summer holiday, so in the meantime we will stop for a week.

下禮拜起,我要上山歇夏,所以暫時停一个月

'Au li-pa chi, ngoo iau zaung san hyih 'au, soo-i dzan z ding ih-kuh nyoeh.

Numerals (數目).

1 一 *ih*
2 二 *nyi*
3 三 *san*
4 四 *s*
5 五 *ng*
6 六 *lok*
7 七 *tshih*
8 八 *pah*
9 九 *kyeu*
10 十 *zeh*
11 十一 *zeh-ih*
12 十二 *zeh-nyi*
13 十三 *zeh-san*
14 十四 *zeh-s*
15 十五 *so-ng*
16 十六 *zeh-lok*
17 十七 *zeh-tshih*
18 十八 *zeh-pah*
19 十九 *zeh-kyeu*
20 念 or 二十 *nyan* or *nyi-seh*
21 念一 *nyan-ih*
22 念二 *nyan-nyi*
23 念三 *nyan-san*
24 念四 *nyan-s*
25 念五 *nyan-ng*
26 念六 *nyan-lok*
27 念七 *nyan-tshih*
28 念八 *nyan-pah*
29 念九 *nyan-kyeu*
30 三十 *san-seh*
31 卅一 *san-zeh-ih*
40 四十 *s-seh*
50 五十 *ng-seh*
60 六十 *lok-seh*
70 七十 *tshih-seh*
80 八十 *pah-seh*
90 九十 *kyeu-seh*
100 一百 *ih-pak*
101 一百零一 *ih-pak ling ih*
102 一百零二 *ih-pak ling nyi*
103 一百零三 *ih-pak ling san*
104 一百零四 *ih-pak ling s*
105 一百零五 *ih-pak ling ng*
106 一百零六 *ih-pak ling lok*
107 一百零七 *ih-pak ling tshih*
108 一百零八 *ih-pak ling pah*

109 一百零九 *ih-pak ling kyeu*
110 一百十 *ih-pak zeh*
111 一百十一 *ih-pak zeh-ih*
200 二百 *nyi-pak*
300 三百 *san-pak*
400 四百 *s-pak*
500 五百 *ng-pak*
600 六百 *lok-pak*
700 七百 *tshih-pak*
800 八百 *pah-pak*
900 九百 *kyeu-pak*

1,000 一千 *ih-tshien*
1,001 一千零零一 *ih-tshien ling ling ih*
2,000 二千 *nyi-tshien*
5,000 五千 *ng-tshien*
10,000 一萬 *ih-man* (or *ih van*)
20,000 二萬 *nyi-man*
50,000 五萬 *ng-man*
100,000 十萬 *zeh-man*
500,000 五十萬 *ng-zeh man*
900,000 九十萬 *kyeu-seh man*
1,000,000 一百萬 *ih-pak man*

Classifiers.

In this and the following sections a number of useful words are grouped according to grammatical or topical divisions. A study of the words, called classifiers, which come between "a" or "an" (or rather its equivalent, the numeral 一 *ih*) and the word itself, will make our communications to the Chinese correct and more lucid.

First Classifier, 个 (*kuh*).

A man. 一个人 *Ih-kuh nyung.*	A bottle. 一个玻璃瓶 *Ih-kuh poo-li-bing.*
A woman. 一个女人 *Ih-kuh nyui-nyung.*	An egg. 一个蛋 *Ih-kuh-dan.*
A son. 一个兒子 *Ih-kuh nyi-ts.*	A scholar. 一个學生子 *Ih-kuh 'auh-sang-ts.*
A daughter. 一个囡 *Ih-kuh noen.*	A farmer. 一个種田入 *Ih-kuh tsoong-dien-nyung.*
A friend. 一个朋友 *Ih-kuh bang-yeu.*	A carpenter. 一个木匠 *Ih-kuh mok-ziang.*

A native.
一个本地人
Ih-kuh pung-di-nyung.

A servant.
一个用人
Ih-kuh yoong-nyung.

A mason.
一个泥水匠
Ih-kuh nyi-s-ziang.

Second Classifier, 隻 (*tsak*).

A dog.
一隻狗
Ih-tsak keu.

A cat.
一隻猫
Ih-tsak mau.

A fowl.
一隻雞
Ih-tsak kyi.

A bird.
一隻鳥
Ih-tsak tiau.

A table.
一隻檯子
Ih-tsak de-ts.

A trunk.
一隻箱子
Ih-tsak siang-ts.

A bed.
一隻床
Ih-tsak zaung.

A plate.
一隻盆子
Ih-tsak bung-ts.

A saucer.
一隻茶杯
Ih-tsak dzo-pe.

A cup.
一隻杯子
Ih-tsak pe-ts.

A stove.
一隻火爐
Ih-tsak hoo-loo.

A watch.
一隻表
Ih-tsak piau.

Third Classifier, 把 (*po*).

A chair.
一把椅子
Ih-po iui-ts.

A fan.
一把扇子
Ih-po sen-ts.

A hammer. 一把榔頭 *Ih-po laung-deu.*	An umbrella. 一把傘 *Ih-po san.*

Fourth Classifier, 條 (*diau*).

A stream. 一條河 *Ih-diau 'oo.*	A rope. 一條繩 *Ih-diau zung.*
A bridge. 一條橋 *Ih-diau jau.*	A snake. 一條蛇 *Ih-diau zo.*
A road. 一條路 *Ih-diau loo.*	A bar of iron. 一條鐵條 *Ih-diau thih-diau.*

Fifth Classifier, 根 (*kung*).

A stick of timber. 一根木頭 *Ih-kung mok-deu.*	A thread. 一根線 *Ih-kung sien.*
A bamboo. 一根竹頭 *Ih-kung tsok-deu.*	A rope. 一根繩 *Ih-kung zung.*

Sixth Classifier, 本 (*pung*).

A book. 一本書 *Ih-pung su.*

Seventh Classifier, 部 (*boo*).

A work of one or more volumes. 一部書 *Ih-boo su.*	A ricksha. 一部東洋車 *Ih-boo toong-yang-tsho.*

A carriage. 一部馬車 *Ih-boo mo-tsho.*	A wheelbarrow. 一部小車 *Ih-boo siau-tsho.*

EIGHTH CLASSIFIER, 座 (*zoo*).

A mountain. 一座山 *Ih-dzoo san.*	A house. 一座房子 *Ih-dzoo vaung-ts.*
A city. 一座城 *Ih-dzoo dzung.*	A pagoda. 一座塔 *Ih-dzoo thah.*

NINTH CLASSIFIER, 疋 (*phih*).

A piece of cloth. 一疋布 *Ih-phih poo.*

TENTH CLASSIFIER, 匹 (*phih*).

A horse. 一匹馬 *Ih-phih mo.*	A mule. 一匹騾子 *Ih-phih loo-ts.*

ELEVENTH CLASSIFIER, 塊 (*khwe*).

A piece of wood. 一塊木頭 *Ih-khwe mok-deu.*	A pane of glass. 一塊玻璃 *Ih-khwe poo-li.*
A slice of meat. 一塊肉 *Ih-khwe nyok.*	A dollar. 一塊洋錢 *Ih-khwe yang-dien.*
A piece of land. 一塊地皮 *Ih-khwe di-bi.*	A brick. 一塊碌磚 *Ih-khwe lok-tsen.*

TWELFTH CLASSIFIER, 幅 (*fok*).

A painting or engraving. 一幅畫圖 *Ih-fok wo-doo.*	A chart or map. 一幅地圖 *Ih-fok di-doo.*

THIRTEENTH CLASSIFIER, 扇 (*sen*).

A door. 一扇門 *Ih-sen mung.*	A screen. 一扇屏風 *Ih-sen bing-foong.*

FOURTEENTH CLASSIFIER, 乘 (*dzung*).

A flight of stairs or a ladder. 一乘扶梯 *Ih-dzung voo-thi.*	A step of a door. 一乘踏步 *Ih-dzung dah-boo.*

FIFTEENTH CLASSIFIER, 頂 (*ting*).

A sedan chair. 一頂轎子 *Ih-ting jau-ts.*	A hat. 一頂帽子 *Ih-ting mau-ts.*

SIXTEENTH CLASSIFIER, 位 (*we*).

A visitor, a customer. 一位客人 *Ih-we khak-nyung.*	A teacher. 一位先生 *Ih-we sien-sang.*

SEVENTEENTH CLASSIFIER, 張 (*tsang*).

A sheet of paper. 一張紙 *Ih-tsang ts.*	A newspaper. 一張新聞紙 *Ih-tsang sing-vung-ts.*

EIGHTEENTH CLASSIFIER, 爿 (*ban*).

A foreign firm. 一爿洋行 *Ih-ban yang-'aung.*	A shop. 一爿店 *Ih-ban tien.*

Nineteenth Classifier, 副 (*foo*).

A set of buttons. 一副鈕子 *Ih-foo nyeu-ts.*	A pair of scrolls. 一副對聯 *Ih-foo te-lien.*

Twentieth Classifier, 雙 (*saung*).

A pair of shoes. 一雙鞋子 *Ih-saung 'a-ts.*	A pair of gloves. 一雙手套 *Ih-saung seu-thau.*

Twenty-first Classifier, 尊 (*tsung*).

An idol. 一尊菩薩 *Ih tsung boo sah.*

Twenty-second Classifier, 包 (*pau*).

A parcel. 一包 *Ih-pau.*	A bale of cotton. 一包棉花 *Ih-pau mien-hwo.*
A bundle of clothing. 一包衣裳 *Ih-pau i-zaung.*	A bale of silk. 一包絲 *Ih-pau s.*

Twenty-third Classifier, 棵 (*khoo*).

A tree. 一棵樹 *Ih khoo zu.*	A flowering plant. 一棵花 *Ih khoo hwo.*

Twenty-fourth Classifier, 面 (*mien*).

A mirror. 一面鏡子 *Ih-mien kyung-ts.*	A flag. 一面旗 *Ih-mien ji*

TWENTY-FIFTH CLASSIFIER, 堆 (*te*).

A pile of fuel. 一堆柴 *Ih te za.*	A pile of stones. 一堆石頭 *Ih te zak-deu.*
A pile of coal. 一堆煤 *Ih te me.*	A pile of goods. 一堆貨色 *Ih te hoo-suh.*

TWENTY-SIXTH CLASSIFIER, 綑 (*khwung*).

A bundle of rice straw. 一綑稻柴 *Ih khwung dau-za.*	A bundle of wood. 一綑柴 *Ih khwung za.*

TWENTY-SEVENTH CLASSIFIER, 管 (*kwen*).

A pen. 一管筆 *Ih kwen pih.*	A foot rule. 一管尺 *Ih kwen tshak.*

TWENTY-EIGHTH CLASSIFIER, 對 (te).

A pair of fowls. 一對雞 *Ih te kyi.*	A husband and wife. 一對夫妻 *Ih te foo-tshi.*

TWENTY-NINTH CLASSIFIER, 口 (*kheu*).

A book-case. 一口書廚 *Ih kheu su-dzu.*	A well. 一口井 *Ih kheu-tsing.*

THIRTIETH CLASSIFIER, 桶 *doong*).

A barrel of flour. 一桶干麵 *Ih doong koen-mien.*	A bucket of water. 一桶水 *Ih doong-s.*

Thirty-first Classifier, 瓶 (*bing*)

A bottle (bottleful). 一瓶 *Ih bing.*	A bottle of medicine. 一瓶藥 *Ih bing yak.*

Thirty-second Classifier, 箱 (*siang*).

A box of tea. 一箱茶葉 *Ih siang dzo-yih.*	A box of materials. 一箱貨色 *Ih siang hoo-suh.*

Thirty-third Classifier, 封 (*foong*).

A letter. 一封信 *Ih foong sing.*

Thirty-fourth Classifier, 帮 (*paung*).

The literary class. 讀書帮 *Dok-su paung.*	The Canton guild. 廣東帮 *Kwaung-toong paung.*
The mercantile class. 生意帮 *Sang-i paung.*	The Ningpo guild. 甯波帮 *Nyung-poo paung* or *Nyung pok paung.*

Thirty-fifth Classifier, 回 (*we*).

One time. 一回 *Ih we.*

Thirty-sixth Classifier, 票 (*phiau*).

A job of work. 一票生活 *Ih phiau sang-weh.*	A business transaction. 一票生意 *Ih phiau sang-i.*

Thirty-seventh Classifier, 椿 (*tsaung*).

An affair. 一椿事體 *Ih tsaung z-thi.*

THIRTY-EIGHTH CLASSIFIER, 層 (*dzung*).

A three-storied house. 三層樓 *San-dzung leu.*	A seven-storied pagoda. 七層塔 *Tshih-dzung thak.*

THIRTY-NINTH CLASSIFIER, 藏 (*dzaung*).

A pile of books. 一藏書 *Ih-dzaung su.*	A pile of plates. 一藏盆子 *Ih-dzaung bung-ts.*

FORTIETH CLASSIFIER, 股 (*koo*).

One share. 一股 *Ih koo.*	A business of three partners. 三股分頭 *San koo vung-deu.*

FORTY-FIRST CLASSIFIER, 間 (*kan*).

One room. 一間 *Ih kan.*	An office. 寫字間 *Sia-z-kan.*
A bed-room. 房間，房頭 *Vaung-kan, vaung-deu.*	Shroff's room. 帳房間 *Tsang-vaung-kan.*

FORTY-SECOND CLASSIFIER, 件 (*jien*).

A garment. 一件衣裳 *Ih jien i-zaung.*	An affair. 一件實體 *Ih jien z-thi.*

FORTY-THIRD CLASSIFIER, 埭 (*da*).

A row of houses. 一埭房子 *Ih da vaung-ts.*	A row of trees. 一埭樹 *Ih da zu.*

Pronouns.

Personal Pronouns.

I.	我	*Ngoo.*	We.	伲	*Nyi.*
You.	儂	*Noong.*	You.	倻	*Na.*
He.	伊	*Yi.*	They.	伊拉	*Yi-la.*

Interrogative Pronouns.

Who? What?
啥 *Sa?*

Which.
那裡 *'a-li.*

Demonstrative Pronouns.

This, these.
第个 *Di-kuh.*

That, those.
伊个 *I-kuh.*

Indefinite Pronouns.

All.
攏總 *Loong-tsoong.*

Many.
多化 *Too-hau.*

Few.
少 *Sau.*

Each.
每 *'Me.*

Whichever.
隨便 *Dzoe-bien.*

Other.
別个 *Bih-kuh.*

Examples of Adjectives.

Good. 好 *Hau.*

Better. 奸點 *Hau-tien.*

Best. 頂好 *Ting-hau.*

Bad. 勿好 *'Veh-hau* (or 怺 *Cheu.*)

Cold. 冷 *Lang.*

Hot. 熱 *Nyih.*

Black. 黑 *Huh.*

White. 白 *Bak.*

Red. 紅 *'Oong.*

Green. 綠 *Lok.*

Blue. 藍 *Lan.*

Yellow. 黃 *Waung.*

Long. 長 *Dzang.*

Short. 短 *Toen.*

High. 高 *Kau.*

Low. 低 *Ti.*

Broad. 闊 *Khweh.*

Narrow. 狹 *'Ah.*

Adverbs.

How. 那能 *Na-nung.*

Why? 爲啥 *We-sa?*

When? 幾時 *Kyi-z?*

Now. 現在 *Yien-dze.*

Thus. 實蓋 *Zeh-ke.*

But. 但是 *Dan-z.*

Only. 不過 *Peh-koo.*

Very. 蠻 *Man.*

Conjunctions.

And. 咾 *Lau.*

Therefore. 所以 *Soo-i.*

Because. 因爲 *Iung-we.*

If. 若是 *Zak-z.*

Then. 難末 *Nan-meh*

Either. 或是 *'Ok-z.*

Directions (方向).

East. 東 *Toong.*	Above. 上頭 *Zaung-deu.*
South. 南 *Nen.*	Below. 下頭 *'Au-deu.*
West. 西 *Si.*	Upstairs. 樓上 *Leu-laung.*
North. 北 *Pok.*	Downstairs. 樓下 *Leu-'au.*
South-east. 東南 *Toong-nen.*	Inside. 裡向 *Li-hyang.*
North-west. 西北 *Si-pok.*	Outside. 外頭 *Nga-deu*
South-west. 西南 *Si-nen.*	In front. 前頭 or 前面 *Zien-deu* or *Zien-mien.*
North-east. 東北 *Toong-pok.*	At the back. 後頭 or 背後 *'Eu-deu* or *Pe-'eu.*
Here. 第頭 or 此地 *Di-deu* or *Ths-di.*	Beside. 傍邊 *Baung-pien.*
There. 伊頭 *I-deu.*	Left. 左邊 *Tsi-pien.*
Where. 那裡 *'A-li*	Right. 右邊 *Yeu-pien.*

In addition to the directions given in the sections, "On the Street"; "The Merchant"; "House Boy and Coolie," etc., the following may prove useful:—

International Banking Corporation.

花旗銀行

Hwo-ji nyung-'aung.

Imperial Bank of China.

中國通商銀行

Tsoong-kok thoong saung nyung-'aung.

Yokohama Specie Bank.

正金銀行

Tsung-kyung nyung-'aung.

Russo-Chinese Bank.

華俄道勝銀行

Wo ngoo dau sung nyung-'aung.

Chartered Bank of India, Australia and China.

麥加利銀行

Mah-ka-li nyung-'aung.

The Missionary Home,

教士公所

Kyau-z koong-soo.

The Palace Hotel.

滙中 *We-tsoong.*

The Hotel Des Colonies.

蜜采里 *Mih-tshe-li.*

The Great Northern Telegraph Company.

大北電報公司

Da-pok dien-pau koong-s.

The Imperial Chinese Telegraph Administration.

中國電報總局

Tsoong-koh dien-pau tsoong-jok.

Eastern Extension Australasia and China Telegraph Co., Ltd.

大東電報公司

Da-toong dien-pau koong-s.

Commercial Pacific Cable Company.

太平洋商務電報公司

Tha-bing-yang saung-woo dien-pau koong-s.

Titles or Designations (稱 呼) .

Parents.
爺娘 *Ya-nyang.*

Father.
爺 *Ya.*

Mother.
娘 *Nyang.*

Husband.
丈夫 *Dzang-foo.*

Wife.
娘子 *Nyang-ts.*

Brother.
弟兄 *Di-hyoong.*

Elder brother.
阿哥 *Ak-koo.*

Younger brother.
兄弟 *Hyoong-di.*

Sister.
姊妹 *Tsi-me.*

Elder sister.
阿姊 *Ah-tsi.*

Younger sister.
妹妹 *Me-me.*

Children.
小囝 *Siau-noen.*

Son.
兒子 *Nyi-ts.*

Daughter.
囡 *Noen.*

Teacher.
先生 *Sien-sang.*

Master.
東家 *Toong-ka.*

Mistress.
東家娘娘 *Toong-ka-nyang-nyang.*

Employé.
夥計 *Hoo-kyi.*

Servant.
用人 *Yoong-nyung.*

Scholar.
學生子 *'Auh-sang-ts.*

Friend.

朋友 *Bang-yeu.*

Neighbor.

鄰舍 *Ling-so.*

Mate or companion.

同事 or 同伴 *Doong-z,* or *Doong-be.*

Cook.

大司務 *Da-s-voo.*

Boy.

細崽 *Si-tse*

Coolie.

苦力 or 出店

Khoo-lih or *Tsheh-tien.*

Amah.

阿媽 *Ak-ma.*

Mafoo.

馬夫 *Mo-foo.*

Rickshaman.

車夫 *Tsho-foo.*

Gardener.

種花園个 *Tsoong-hwo-yoen-kuh.*

Relative.

親眷 *Tshing-kyoen.*

Washerman.

淨衣裳个 *Zing-i-zaung-kuh.*

Tailor.

裁縫 *Ze-voong.*

Carpenter.

木匠 *Mok-ziang.*

Mason.

坭水匠 *Nyi-s-ziang*

Blacksmith.

鐵匠 *Thih-ziang.*

Coppersmith.

銅匠 *Doong-ziang.*

Silversmith.

銀匠 *Nyung-ziang.*

Shoemaker.

鞋匠 or 做鞋子个 *'A-ziang* or *Tsoo 'a-ts kuh.*

Baker.

做饅頭个 *Tsoo-men-deu-kuh.*

Weather (天 氣).

To-day the weather is fine.
今朝天氣蠻好
Kyung-tsau thien-chi 'man-hau.

To-day is dark.
今朝天色陰暗
Kyung-tsau thien-suh iung-en.

Perhaps it will rain.
恐怕要落雨
Khoong-pho iau lauh-yui.

The wind is high.
有大風
Yeu doo foong.

To-day is very warm.
今朝蠻熱
Kyung-tsau 'man nyih.

Yesterday was very cold.
昨日邉冷
Zauh-nyih 'man lang.

Perhaps to-morrow will be fine.
明朝或者會天好 [or 天晴]
Ming-tsau 'ok-tse we thien-hau [or *thien-dzing.*]

There has been too much rain.
雨水忒多
Yui-s thuh-too.

It looks like snow.
要落雪
Iau lauh sih.

To-day there is frost.
今朝有霜
Kyung-tsau yeu saung.

To-day there is ice.
今朝有冰
Kyung-tsau yeu ping.

It is foggy outside.
外頭有霧露
Nga-deu yeu 'oo-loo.

It is stormy.
有大風雨
Yeu doo foong-yui.

House Vocabulary.

Basin.

面盆 *Mien-bung.*

Bath room.

淨浴間 *Zing-yok kan.*

Bath tub.

浴缸 or 浴盆 *Yok-kaung*, or *yok-bung.*

Bath tray.

浴缸座盤 *Yok-kaung dzoo-ben.*

Bamboo screen.

竹簾 *Tsok-lien.*

Bed-room.

房間 *Vaung-kan.*

Bell.

鈴 *Ling.*

Bed.

床 *Zaung.*

Book-case.

書厨 *Su-dzu.*

Broom.

掃箒 *Sau-tseu.*

Carpet.

地毯 *Di-than.*

Chair.

椅子 *Iui-ts.*

Clock.

鐘 *Tsoong.*

Clothes horse.

衣架 *I ka.*

Coal-house.

煤間 *Me kan.*

Coal scuttle.

煤桶 *Me-doong.*

Coal shovel.

煤抄 *Me-tshau.*

Commode.

馬桶 *Mo-doong.*

Boiler (for water).
水鍋 *S-koo.*

Dining-room.
吃飯間 *Chuh-van-kan.*

Draught screen.
屏風 *Bing-foong.*

Dressing room.
著衣間 *Tsak-i kan.*

Filter.
沙漏氷缸 *So-loo-s kaung.*

Flower glass.
花瓶 *Hwo-bing.*

Flower pot.
花盆 *Hwo-bung.*

Frying pan.
熬盆 *Ngau bung.*

Garden.
花園 *Hwo-yoen.*

Hall or lobby.
過路間 *Koo-loo-kan.*

Key.
鑰匙 *Yak-dz.*

Kitchen.
燒飯間 *Sau-van-kan.*

Dog kennel.
狗棚 *Keu bang.*

Lock.
鎖 *Soo.*

Looking glass.
鏡子 *Kyung-ts.*

Native delf basins.
罐頭 *Kwen-deu.*

Nursery.
小囝房間 *Siau-noen vaung-kan.*

Organ.
風琴 *Foong-jung.*

Ornaments.
裝飾个物事 *Tsaung-seh kuh meh-z.*

Parlour or Drawing room.
客堂間 *Khah-daung-kan.*

Piano.
洋琴 *Yang-jung.*

Pictures.
畫圖 *Wo-doo.*

Rolling pin or roller.
麵杖 or 桿筒 *Mien-dzang,* or *koen-doong.*

Saucepan.
鑊子 or 鐵鍋 *'Auh-ts,* or *thih-koo.*

Scales (foreign).
磅秤 *Paung-tshung.*

Scales, Chinese wooden steelyards.
天平 *Thien-bing.*

Scrubbing brush.
刷箒 or 筅箒 *Suh-tseu*, or *sien-tseu.*

Sideboard.
落菜檯 *Lok-tshe-de.*

Sieve.
綳篩 *Pang-s.*

Soap dish.
肥皂缸 *Bi-zau-kaung.*

Stable.
馬棚間 *Mo-bang-kan.*

Stairway.
扶梯間 *Voo-thi-kan.*

Store room.
伙食間 *Hoo-zuh-kan.*

Study.
讀書間 *Dok-su-kan.*

Table.
檯子 *De-ts.*

Table cover.
檯布 *De-poo.*

Tub or foot bath.
脚桶 *Kyak-doong.*

Verandah.
洋檯 or 走廊 *Yang-de*, or *tseu-laung.*

Wardrobe.
衣厨 *I-dzu.*

Washstand.
揩面檯 *Kha-mien-de.*

Water jug.
水瓶 or 水壺 *S-bing*, or *s-'oo.*

Water-closet.
坑棚間 *Khang-bang-kan.*

Watering can or pot.
噴桶 *Phung-doong.*

Writing desk.
寫字檯 *Sia-z-de.*

Time (時候).

This year.
今年 *Kyung-nyien.*

Last year.
舊年 *Jeu-nyien.*

Next year.
開年 or 明年 *Khe-nyien*, or *ming-nyien.*

New year.
新年 *Sing-nyien.*

This month.
第个月 *Di-kuh nyoeh.*

Last month.
上个月 or 前月 *Zaung-kuh nyoeh*, or *Zien-nyoeh.*

Next month.
下个月 or 下月 *'Au-kuh nyoeh*, or *'Au nyoeh.*

To-day.
今朝 *Kyung-tsau.*

Day before yesterday.
前日 *Zien-nyih.*

Day after to-morrow.
後日 *'Eu-nyih.*

A few days.
勿多幾日 *'Veh-too kyi nyih.*

A week.
一禮拜 *Ih li-pa.*

Sunday.
禮拜日 *Li-pa-nyih.*

Monday.
禮拜一 *Li-pa-ih.*

Tuesday.
禮拜二 *Li-pa-nyi.*

Wednesday.
禮拜三 *Li-pa-san.*

To-morrow.
明朝 *Ming-tsau.*

Yesterday.
昨日 *Zauh-nyih.*

Saturday.
禮拜六 *Li-pa-lok.*

One hour.
一點鐘 *Ih tien-tsoong.*

Half hour.
半點鐘 *Pen tien-tsoong.*

Quarter hour.
一刻 *Ih khuh.*

A minute.
一分 *Ih fung.*

A second.
一秒 *Ih miau.*

A quarter past 2 o'clock.
兩點一刻 *Liang tien ih khuh.*

Half-past 3 o'clock.
三點半 *San tien pen.*

A quarter to 4 o'clock.
四點缺一刻 or 三點三刻
S tien choeh ih khuh, or *San tien san khuh.*

Five minutes past four o'clock.
四點過五分 *S tien koo ng fung.*

Thursday.
禮拜四 *Li-pa-s.*

Friday.
禮拜五 *Li-pa-ng.*

Morning.
早晨 *Tsau-zung.*

Forenoon.
上半日 *Zaung-pen-nyih.*

Afternoon.
下半日 *'Au-pen-nyih.*

Mid-day.
日中 *Nyih-tsoong.*

Evening.
夜快 *Ya-khwa.*

Night.
夜頭 or 夜裡 *Ya-deu*, or *Ya-li.*

Now.
現在 *Yien-dze.*

Afterward.
後首 *'Eu-seu.*

One time.
一回 *Ih-we.*

Two times, twice.
兩回 *Liang-we.*

Ten minutes to 5 o'clock.

五點缺十分 *Ng tien choeh zeh fung.*

Vocabulary.

A

Above	Zaung-deu
According	Tsau
Account	Tsang
Accounts	Soen-tsang
Affair	Z-thi
Afternoon	‘Au-pen-nyih
Afterwards	‘Eu-seu
Again	Tse
Again	‘eu-seu
Age	Kwe-kang
Age	Soe [soo]
Ague	ngauh-ts
All	Loong-tsoong
Already	I-kyung
Am	Z
Amah	A-ma
American	’Me-kok nyung
American Bank	Hwo-ji nyung-‘aung
Among them	Ne-tsoong
And	Lau
Another	Bik-kuh
Another time	‘au-we
Answer	We-sing

Apples	Bing-koo
Application	Tan
Apricots	Ang-ts
Arrange	Yui-be
Arrived	Tau
Ask	Tshing
Ask	Thau
Aspirate	Tsheh-foong
Astor House	Li-dzo
At	La
At once	Zieu

B

Baby	Siau-noen
Back (go)	We-tseu
Bad	'Veh hau
Bake	Hoong
Bamboo	Tsok-deu
Bank	Nyung-'aung
Basin	Mien-bung
Basket	Lan
Bath tub	Yok-kaung
Beans	Deu
Beans (string)	Tau-deu
Beautiful	Hau khoen
Beautiful	Man hau
Because	We-ts
Because	Iung-we
Bed	Zaung
Bed-room	Vaung-kan
Bedding	Phoo-ke
Beef	Nyeu-nyok
Beginning	Chi-deu
Bell	Ling

Below	‘Au-deu
Beside	Baung pien
Better	Hau-tien
Biboes	Bih-bo
Bird	Tiau
Biscuits	Thah-ping
Biscuits	Ping-koen
Black	Huh
Blacksmith	Thih-ziang
Blow	Ths
Blue	Lan
Boat	Zen
Boil	Zah
Boil	Tung
Boiling water	Khe-s
Book	Su
Book-case	Su-dzu
Bottle	Bing
Boy	Si-tse
Box	Siang-ts
Bread	Men-deu
Brick	Lok-tsen
Bridge	Jau
Bright	Liang
Bring	Nau-le
Bring	Tan-le
British	Da-Iung
Broad	Khweh
Broil	Hyuin
Broken	Wa-theh
Broken	Se
Broom	Sau-tseu
Brother	Di-hyoong
Brush	Seh-tseu
Brush (to)	Seh

Bundle	Pau
Business	Sang-i
Business	Z-thi
Busy	Maung
But	Dan-z
Butter	Na-yeu
Button	Nyeu-ts
Buy, bought	Ma

C

Cabbage	Kyoen-sing-tse
Calf	Siau-nyeu
Call	Tshing
Call	Kyau
Can	Khau-i
Candle	Lali-tsok
Cannot	'Veh-nung
Careful	Taung-sing
Carpenter	Mok-ziang
Carpet	Di-than
Carriage	Mo-tsho
Carrots	'Oong lau-bok
Carvings	Khuh-tsauh
Cat	Mau
Cathedral	'Oong-li-pa-daung
Cauliflower	Hwo-tshe
Cent	Fung
Certainly	Ih-ding
Chair	Iui-ts
Chair (Sedan)	Jau-ts
Change	Wen
Characters	Z
Charcoal	Than
Cheaper	Jang-tien

Chicken	Kyi
Children	Siau-noen
Chimney	Ien-tshoong
China	Dz-chi
China	Tsoong-kok
China Merchants	Tsau-saung-jok
Chinese Post Office	Yeu-tsung-jok
Chit book	Soong-sing-boo
Choked	Suh-meh
Church	Li pa-daung
City	Dzung
Clean	Koen-zing
Cloak	Bau-kwo
Clock	Tsoong
Cloth	Poo
Clothes	I-zaung
Clothes and hat	I-mau
Club, the	Tsoong-we
Coal	Me
Coal scuttle	Me-doong
Coal (soft)	Ien-me
Coal (hard)	Bak-me
Coals	Me
Cold	Lang
Collar	Ling-deu
Colour	Ngan-suh
Come	Le
Come	Tau
Commercial traveller	Teu sang-i kuh
Commode	Mo-doong
Company	‘Aung
Compradore	Tsang-vaung
Compradore	’Ma-ban
Consulate	Koong-kwen
Contrary (tide)	Nyuh-s

Convenient	Bien-taung
Cook	Da s-voo
Cook (to)	Sau
Cooking stove	Thih-tsau
Coolie	Tseh-tien
Coolie	Siau-koong
Coolie	Khoo-lih
Correctly	Te
Cost	Ka-dien
Cost (tow)	(Thoo) dien
Cotton	Mien-hwo
Country	Kok
Cuffs	Zieu-deu
Cup	Pe
Curtains	Tshaung-lien
Custom	Kwe-kyui
Customs	Sing-kwan
Cut	Ngah

D

Dark	Huh
Daughter	Noen
Day	Nyih
Dear	Kyui
Dialect (col.)	Thoo-bak
Dining-room	Chuh-van-kan
Dinner	Ya-van
Dirty	Auh-tshauh
Discharging	Sia-hoo
Discount	Ngah-theh
Distinctly	Tshing-saung
Doctor	I-sang
Dog	Keu
Dollar	Yang-dien

Door	Mung
Down	Tih
Downstairs	Leu-‘au
Draught screen	Bing-foong
Dry	‘Oen
Dry	Koen
Duck	Ah
Dust, to	Toen koen-zing
Duty	Soe
Duty memo	Soe-tan

E

Each	‘Me
Earlier	Tsau-tien
Easier	Khwen-tien
Easily	Yoong-yi
East	Toong
Eat	Chuh
Ebb	The
Eggs	Dan
Either	‘Ok-z
Embroidery	Koo-sieu
England	Iung-kok
Enough	Yeu-tse
Enough	Keu
Evening	Ya-khwa
Exchange	‘Aung-dzing
Exchange	Li-deu
Exchange	Wen
Export	Tsheh-kheu
Extra	Ling-nga

F

Family	Ih ka-mung

Fan	Sen-ts
Farmer	Tsoong-dien-nyung
Father	Ya
Favorable (tide)	Zung-s
Favorable (wind)	Zung-foong
Feed (verb)	Iui
Feed (verb)	Chuh
Feed (noun)	Liau
Fever	Ngauh-ts
Fever	'Oen-nyih
Few	'Veh-too
Few	Sau
Filter	So-loo-s kaung
Find (try to)	Zing
Finish	Tsoo-hau
Finish	Wen
Fire	Hoo
Firewood	Za
First	Sien
First class	Deu-tung
Fish	Ng
Flag	Ji
Flannel	Fah-lan-nyoong
Floor	Di-pan
Flour	Mi-fung
Flour	Koen-mien
Flow	Tsang
Flue	Ien-tshoong
Foggy	'Oo-loo
Food	Chuh-kuh meh-z
Foot	Kyak
Foot rule	Tshak
Foot-stove	Kyak-loo
Foreign	Nga-kok
Forenoon	Zaung-pen-nyih

Forget	Maung-kyi
Fowl	Kyi
French	Fah-kok
French Concession	Fah-tsoo-ka
Frenchman	Fah-kok nyung
Fresh	Dan
Friday	Li-pa-ng
Friend	Bang-yeu
Frost	Saung
Fruits	Koo-ts
Fry	Tsien
Fuel	Za
Furs	Bi-hoo

G

Gardens	Hwo-yoen
German	Tuh-kok nyung
German bank	Tuh-wo nyung-'aung
Get	Zing
Girth	Mo-doo-ta
Give	Peh
Glass	Poo-li
Go	Chi
Go (run)	Bau
Going out	Tsheh-chi
Go (stop)	Ding
Godown	Dzan-vaung
Going away	Tsheh-mung
Gold	Kyung
Good	Hau
Good-bye	Man chi (etc.)
Good morning	Tsau-'a
Goods	Hoo-suh
Goose	Ngoo

Grapes	Beh-dau
Great Lake	Tha-‘oo
Great (much)	Doo
Green	Lok
Greetings	Maung maung
Guests	Khak-nyung

H

Half	Pen
Hammer	Laung-deu
Hangchow	‘Aung-tseu
Harness	Mo ka-sang
Hat	Mau-ts
Have	Yeu
He	Yi
Help	Siang-paung
Here	Di-deu
Here	Ths-di
High	Kau
High	Kyui
Hills	San
Home	Ok-li
Hongkew	‘Oong-kheu
Hongkong & Shanghai Bank	We-foong
Honorable	Kwe
Hood	Boong-poo
Horse	Mo
Hospital	I-yoen
Hot	Nyih
Hot	Khe
Hot	Yaung
Hoteldes Colonies	Mih-tshe-li
Hotel	Khak-nyui
House (home)	Ok-li

House	Vaung-ts
How	Na-nung
How are you?	Hau la va?
How many?	Kyi? Kyi-kuh?
How much?	Kyi-hau?
Humble	Bi
Hurt	Saung
Husband	Dzang-foo

I

I	Ngoo
Ice	Ping
Ice-box	Ping-siang
Idiom	Wo-fah
Idle	Lan-doo
Idol	Boo-sah
If	Zak-z
Ill	Mau-bing
Imperial Customs	Sing-kwan
Imperial P.O.	Yeu-tsung-jok
Import	Tsing-kheu
Important	Iau-kyung
Impossible	Le-'veh-ji
Increase	Ka
Inside	Li-hyang
Interrogative sign	Va?
Iron	Thih
Is	Z

J

Jacket	Mo-kwo
Japan	Tooug-yang
Jar	Peh-deu
Jardine's	Yi-'woo

Jetty	Mo-deu
Jelly	Toong
Just now	Yien-dze

K

Kerosene oil	Hoo-yeu
Kettle	S-‘oo
Key	Yak-dz
Kitchen	Sau-van-kan
Knit	Kyih
Know	Nyung-tuh
Know	Hyau-tuh
Kong	Kaung

L

Labour	Koong-foo
Ladder	Voo-thi
Lamp	Tung
Land	Di-bi
Late	Man
Late	An
Laudah	Lau-da
Lazy	lan-doo
Leak	Leu
Learn	‘Auh
Leave	Ding, li-khe
Leaving	Li-khe
Left	Tsi-pien
Less	Sau
Let	Nyang
Letter	Sing
Lichees	Li-ts
Light (verb)	Tien
Lighter (thinner)	Bok-tien

Listen	Thing
Little	Sau
Lock	Soo
Long	Dzang
Looking glass	Kyung-ts
Loose	Khwen
Loose	Soong
Lost	Seh-theh-tse
Low	Ti
Low (cheap)	Jang
Lowdah	Lau-da
Lower (sail)	Lauh
Lower	‘Au-tien
Luggage	‘Ang-li

M

Mafoo	Mo-foo
Mail	Siug
Make	Tsoo
Mau	Nyung
Mandarin (dialect)	Kwen-wo
Many	Too-hau
Map	Di-doo
Market	Ka-laung
Market	Z-mien
Market	Ka
Marks	Kyi-‘au
Mason	Ni-s-ziang
Master	Toong-ka
Matches	Z-le-hoo
Matters	Z-thi
Me	Ngoo
Meals	Chuli-van
Meat	Nyok

Medicine	Yak
Mend	Sieu
Mend	Poo
Merchant	Sang-i-nyung
Mexican	Iung-yang
Mirror	Kyung-ts
Milk	Nyeu-na
Mine	Ngoo-kuh
Mistake	'Veh te
Mistake	tsho
Missing	Choeh-sau
Missionary	Dzen-dau-kuh
Monday	Li-pa-ih
Money (price)	Ka-dien
Month	Nyoeh
More	Too
More	Too-tien
Morning	Tsau
Morning	Tsau-zung
Mother	Nyang
Much	Too
Mule	Loo-ts
Must	Iau
Mutton (various)	
My	Ngoo-kuh

N

Name	Sing, 'au
Name	Ming-deu
Narrow	'Ah
Native	Pung-di
Neighbor	Ling-so
Newspaper	Sing-vung-ts
New	Sing-kuh

New year	Sing-nyien
Next	‘Au
Next	Kah-pih
Next year	Khe-nyien
Next week	‘Au-li-pa
Night	Ya-deu
Ningpo	Nyung-poo
North	Pok
Not	’Veh
Now	Yien-dze

O

Oatmeal	Da-mak-fung
O’clock	Tien-tsoong
Office	Sia-z kan
Officer	Ban z kuh
Oil (Kerosene)	Hoo-yeu
Old	Lau
Oldest	Ting-doo kuh
Only	Tsuh-yeu
Only	Peh-koo
Open	Khe
Opinion	I-s
Opium	Ia-phien-ien
Oranges	Kyoeh-ts
Or	‘Ok-z
Order	Ding
Organ	Foong-jung
Other	Bih-kuh
Out	Nga-deu
Outlay	Fi-yoong
Outside	Nga deu

P

Pagoda	Thah
Paid	Foo
Paid	Wen
Painting	Wo-doo
Paper	Ts
Parcel	Pau
Parents	Ya-nyang
Pass	Pha-s
Pass-book	Boo-ts
Pattern	Yang-ts
Pattern	Yang-suh
Pay	Be
Pay	Foo
Peaches	Dau-ts
Pen	Pih
People	Nyung
Perhaps	Khoong-pho
Pheasant	Ya-kyi
Piano	Yang-jung
Picture	Wo-doo
Piece	Jien
Pile	Ih te
Pine apple	Poo-loo-mih
Place	Di-faung
Plant	Hwo
Plate	Bung-ts
Please	Tshing
Pocket	De
Police Office	Dzing-boo-vaung
Pony	Mo
Pootung	Phoo-toong
Post Office	Su-sing-kwen
Pot	‘Oo

Pound	Paung
Prepare	Yui-be
Presently	Zieu
Price	Ka-dien
Promise	Iung-hyui
Proper	Iung-ke-kuh
Proper	Kwe-kyui
Properly	Hau
Pumelo	Vung-tan
Purchase	Ma
Purchasing	Ma
Put	Pa
Put	Faung
Put on	Tsak
Put-up	Tsaung
Put-up	Faung-‘au-chi

Q

Quarter	Ih khuh
Quicker	Khwa-tien
Quickly	Khwa-tien

R

Rain	Yui, yui-s
Raining	Lauh-yui
Raise (sail)	Tsha
Read	Dok
Ready?	Hau-me?
Real	Tsung-kuh
Receive	Seu
Recently	Jung-le
Red	‘Oong
Re-export	Tsen-kheu
Relative	Tshing-kyoen

Repair	Sieu
Require	Yoong
Return (back)	We-tsen-chi
Return home	Kyui chi
Rice	Mi
Rice straw	Dau-za
Ricksha	Toong-yang-tsho
Rickshaman	Tsho-foo
Right	Yeu-pien
Right (correct)	Te kuh
Right (correct)	'Veh tsho
Rising	Tsang
Road	Loo
Roast	Hoong
Roll up	Tang-chi-le
Room	Vaung-ts
Room	Kan
Rope	Zung
Rug	Than-ts
Run away	Dau-tseu
Russian	Ngoo-kok

S

Saddle (verb)	Tsaung
Saddle (noun)	Oen-ts
Sail	Boong
Salt (noun)	Yien
Salt (adj.)	'An
Same	Tsho-'veh-too
Sample	Yang-ts
Saturday	Li-pa-lok
Saucer	Dzo-pe
Say	Wo
Scales	Paung-tshung

Scholar	'Auh-sang-ts
Scour	Tshah
Screen	Bing-foong
Scrolls	Te-lien
Scull	Yau
Second	Miau
Sedan chair	Jau-ts
Sell	Ma-theh
Servant	Yoong-nyung
Sew	Voong
Shake	Teu-teu
Shanghai	Zaung-he
Share	Koo
Shilling	Sien-ling
Ship	Zen
Shirt	'Oen-san
Shoemaker	'A-ziang
Shoes	'A-ts
Shop	Tien
Short	Toen
Shoulders	Kyien-paung
Shoulders	Kyung-kweh
Shroff	Seu-tsang
Shroff	Seli-lau-fu
Shut	Kwan
Sick	Sang-bing
Sieve	Pang-s
Silk	S-dzeu
Silver	Nyung
Silversmith	Nyung-ziang
Silver ware	Nyung-chi
Singlet	Tshung-san
Sir	Sien-sang
Sister	Tsi-me
Sit	Zoo

Skirt	Juin
Sleeve	Zieu-ts
Slower	Man-tien
Slowly	Man-le-si
Smoke	Ien
Smoke	Chuh-ien
Snake	Zo
Snipe	Tsok-kyi
Snow	Sih
So	Zeh-ke
So	Soo-i
Soap	Bi-zau
Soda	Kan
Solder	'Oeu
Some	Tien
Son	Nyi-ts
Soochow	Soo-tseu
Soon	Zieu
Soup	Thaung
South	Nen
Sovereign	Kyung-yang
Speak	Wo
Spinach	Poo-tshe
Spoiled	Loong-wa
Stairs	Voo-thi
Starch	Tsiang
Start	Khe (zen)
Start	Khe (tsho)
Station	Tsho-dzan
Stay	Ding
Steady	'Wung-taung
Steam	Tsung
Steamer	Lung-zen
Stew	Tung
Stiff	Ngang

Still	Wan
Stockings	Mah
Stones	Zak-deu
Store	Tien
Stop	Ding
Storage	Dzan-tsoo
Stove	Hoo-loo
Straw	Dau-za
Strawberries	Nga-kah yang-me
Stream	‘Oo
Strong	Lau-kuh
Stronger	Hau-tien
Study	Dok-su
Substitute	Thi-koong
Sugar	Daung
Summer	‘Au-thien
Sun	Nyih-deu
Sunday	Li-pa-nyih
Supper	Ya-van
Surname	Sing
Sweep	Sau

T

Table	De-ts
Tailor	Ze-voong
Take (drive)	Tsho
Take (drive)	Soong
Take (drive)	Ta
Take out	Tan tsheh-chi
Take off	Tan-chi
Taken (moved)	Pen
Tea	Dzo
Tea	Dzo-yih
Teacher	Sien-sang

Tea-pot	Dzo-'oo
Tear	Phoo
Tell	Kau-soo
Thanks	Zia-zia
That	I-kuh
There	I-deu
Therefore	Soo-i
Then	Keh-meh
Then	Nan-meh
Thicker	'Eu-tien
Think	Siang
Things	Meh-z
This	Di-kuh
These	Di-we
Those	I-kuh
Thread	Sien
Thursday	Li-pa-s
Thus	Zeh-ke
Tickets	Phiau-ts
Tide	Dzau-s
Tie	Khwung
Tie (noun)	Kyih-ts
Tiffin	Tsoong-van
Tight	Kyung
Timber	Mok-deu
Tired	Sa-doo
To	Tau
Toast (to)	Hoong
To-day	Kyung-tsau
Told	Kau-soo
Too	Thuh
Too late	ThThuh-anuh
Too much	Thuh-doo
To-morrow	Ming-tsau
To-night	Kyung-ya

Ton	Tung
Torn	Loong-wa
Tow	Thoo
Tow	Thoo-chien
Transaction	Sang-i
Tranship	Koo-zen
Tree	Zu
Trousers	Khoo-ts
Trunk	Siang-ts
Tuesday	Li-pa-nyi
Turkey	Hoo-kyi
Turnips	Lau-bok
Twice	Liang-we

U

Umbrella	San
United States	Hwo-ji (see America)
Union Church	Soo-tseu-‘oo li-pa-daung
Until	Tuug
Upstairs	Leu-laung
Use	Yoong

V

Vegetables	Soo-tshe
Verandah	Yang-de
Very	’Man
Very well	’Man-hau
Vet. surgeon	Mo-i
Visitor	Khak-nyung

W

Wages	Koong-dien
Wait	Tung-la

Walk	Tseu
Want	I au
Wardrobe	I-dzu
Wares	Hoo-suh
Warm	Nyih
Wash	Zing
Washers	Nyien-dien
Washerman	Da-i-zaung-kuh
Washerman	Zing-i-zaung-kuh
Washstand	Kha-mien-de
Water	S
Waterproof apron	Yeu-poo
Watch	Piau
Way	Loo
We	Nyi
Weather	Thien-chi
Wednesday	Li-pa-san
Week	Li-pa
Weighing	Dzoong
Well	Hau
Well (noun)	Tsing
West	Si
Wharf	Mo-deu
What	Sa
When	Kyi-z
Where?	'A-li?
Wheels	Lung-ben
Wheelbarrow	Siau-tsho
Which	'A-li
Whichever	Dzoe-bien
White	Bak
Who	Sa?
Why?	We-sa?
Why?	Sa yoen-koo?
Wife	Nyang-ts

Wine	Tsieu
Wind	Foong
Window	Tshaung
Wipe	Kha
Wish	Iau
Woman	Nyui-nyung
Words	Seh-wo
Work	Sang-weh
Worse	Cheu
Wrap	Pau
Write	Sia

Y

Yangtze	Yang-ts
Year	Nyien
Yellow	Waung
Yesterday	Zauh-nyih
Yokohama Specie Bank	Tsung-kyung nyung-'aung
You	Noong
Youngest	Ting-siau-kuh
Your	Noong-kuh
Yulo	Yau

Index.

A

B

C

D

F

H

I

J

K

L

M

N

O

P

S

T

V

W

Y

Z

Printed by Libri Plureos GmbH in Hamburg,
Germany